DIRECT CARVING IN STONE

1. MICHELANGELO.
*Unfinished figure
for projected tomb
of Pope Julius.*
Marble

DIRECT CARVING
IN
STONE

MARK BATTEN
PP.R.B.S., R.B.A.

LONDON / ALEC TIRANTI / 1966

1st edition (Studio Books) 1957
(Stone Sculpture by Direct Carving)
Present revised and enlarged edition 1966

PRINTED BY PORTLAND PRESS LTD
BOUND BY MANSELL & CO LTD, LONDON N.1

CONTENTS

ACKNOWLEDGEMENTS

The author wishes to express his special thanks to Arthur Gardner, F.S.A. for allowing him to use so many illustrations, from his great collection of photographs of medieval work, figures 19-23, 25, 27-29, 73, 78, and to Oliver Batten for the trouble he took with the photographs specially taken for figures 8, 11, 33-35, 37, 38, 45, 49, 51, 55, 56.

For permission to reproduce work, the author also wishes to express his thanks to the President, Trinity College, Oxford; The Librarian, Bodleian Library, Oxford; The Courtauld Institute of Art, figures 74-77; The Trustees, British Museum, figures 7, 18, 30, 31, 62-66, 77; The Trustees, British Museum (Natural History) fig. 6; The Trustees, Tate Gallery, figures 68, 79; The Victoria and Albert Museum, figures 24, 32, 67; and to Bath and Portland Group Ltd. (photos: Herbert of Weymouth) figures 57-59.

Also to John Grundy who kindly supplied the photographs reproduced in figures 17, 12, 46, and who helped with the diagram in figure 16; and to Alinari for figures 1, 91, 92, 93.

CHAPTER ONE

CONSIDERING SCULPTURE IN GENERAL
AND
STONE SCULPTURE IN PARTICULAR

Concerned as I am with sculpture and all related matters, I am frequently brought up short by surprise at how much less the public knows about this art than about other forms of art. Furthermore, this seems to be so even with those people who do have an interest of a general kind in the visual arts, and, moreover, even with many art students who are not actually sculpture students. For instance, most people going round an art exhibition seem to know if they are looking at, say, an oil painting, or a water colour, or a print. Yet, how few seem to recognize the basic differences between, for instance, a work cast in bronze or other metal, or one carved in stone, or one built up by welding metal parts, or even one in the temporary plaster of paris state, if it is coloured.

Surprise at this being so is warranted, if for no better reason, at least by the fact that sculpture is the form of art most frequently confronting people in their daily lives; certainly if they live in or visit cities. There are not many journeys, even short ones, that can be made in a city without seeing some sculpture, either free standing statues, or works incorporated in buildings. While to see art in its other forms one must usually seek it out by visiting a gallery. Nor is this surprising lack of knowledge about the art of sculpture simply the product of a special degree of indifference on the part of the public to this form of art in particular. The contrary seems to be the case. For instance, Sir Winston Churchill, that man with such exceptional talent for understanding the attitudes of the British public, had something to say in confirmation of this point. Lord Eccles (at that time Sir David Eccles) related, that on assuming the office of Minister of Works, he visited his Prime Minister, Sir Winston Churchill. The items of good advice the great man gave him included the following, 'Never forget to beware of meddling with statues in public places. They can be like dynamite.' Since, in general, feeling is manifestly not less strong about sculpture than about other forms of the visual arts one would expect it to follow that knowledge about

1

sculpture would not be less. Yet, paradoxically, we find that it is much less.

In the field of sculpture, furthermore, the kind of material and the way it is manipulated to produce the work has a more characterizing influence on the quality of the resulting work than these elements do in the field of painting and the allied techniques. Thus it is necessary that indeed more, not less, should be understood about the materials and methods of sculpture by the person who wants to have a comprehensive appreciation of the visual arts. Nor is this point invalidated, but made stronger rather, by the degree of overlapping between the techniques of sculpture and of painting which has developed in recent years.

Going on from the proposition that sculpture is that art in which the combination of material and technique chosen, as the best one for the realization of the artist's conception, will have the most marked influence on the character of the work produced, we see the paramount necessity for intensive study of this aspect. Considering sculptors, past and present, we find that the respective temperament of each one draws him magnetically to a particular material-technique-group sympathetic to his nature. While explorations have, of course, to be made for him to find out what this is, as a rule he settles down in one field fairly soon. Every possibility seems to be worked out somewhere in life producing the exceptional case, but the main trend is for each sculptor to work increasingly in a particular material-technique-group which is the most sympathetic to the kind of ideas he wants to develop. This takes place to a greater degree here than in the other forms of the visual arts. It is not denied that there are extreme examples on both sides and degrees between but this does not invalidate the general conclusion. This view has the support of the classic example of Michelangelo, exponent par excellence of the extreme attitude.

For him, sculpture was something made exclusively of one material and by only one method. And this, in spite of the fact that he was forced by other people to spend quite a lot of his life not doing sculpture at all, but doing painting. It is easy to multiply examples of great or good sculptors of this attitude or akin to it. Conversely, it is difficult to present many examples of great sculptors to whom any material and technique are equally compatible without preference; to whom sculpture is merely an idea put into three dimensions and not especially made of any particular substance or by any particular method.

2

Let it not be thought that I attach less importance than anyone else does to the fundamental role occupied by the relationships and the proportions between the forms and the different parts of the forms in a work of art. Nor let it be thought that I attach less importance than others do to the relationships between the filled volumes and the spatial outer embracing volumes integrated into a design. But to make a work fully interpret each sculptor's special illumination of life to these things must be added those others upon which it is the purpose of this book to focus more attention than is elsewhere brought to bear. For instance, an entirely different impact is made upon the spectator by the suave and stately masses embodied in a hard stone not elaborately fretted in contrast with an assemblage of steel rods and wires jaggedly welded together. It must be obvious that there are things that cannot be expressed in both of these two diverse fields of operation but each only in the one. This is not to say that stone cannot be made to go a long way towards the second mood nor welded steel sheet towards the first when the need arises. Nevertheless each main current is in a fundamentally different direction and generally a man is, by temperament, impelled in one of these directions, but not both.

Since the material and the technique play such a decisive role in imparting to a sculpture an all pervading quality or characteristic flavour, specialization is finally inevitable to bring about the fulfilment of personality. The temperament of each particular sculptor will find its proper expression only in one special type of the groupings of textures, surfaces, characteristic forms and even tones or colours. Only the degree of diversity within which each can find fulfilment will be the varying factor between man and man. It will vary from the extreme and purist attitude of a Michelangelo to that bordering on the attitude of the accommodation man. By accommodation man, I mean one without convictions or genuine feelings, but one who does with talent and skill, whatever type of thing the fashion of the day, or the wants of a client, calls for.

Should it be thought that I tend to attribute relatively too much importance to the involvement of material and technique in the process by which an artist expresses himself, it is only necessary for me to direct attention to actual sculptures rather than arguments. For illustration, it is not in many cases that a person experienced in the field of art cannot quickly name the sculptor of any individual work seen for the first time in a case where that sculptor's work is in general known to him. This, in the final analysis, is because the sculptor's personality and temperament sings out from the work through the choice of material and the manner in which it is manipulated to carry out the purpose which his kind of ideas demand. This will be general to all his work, an innate product of his personality, to which will be added the particular statement which the individual work has been created to voice. Is it not this aspect which is fixed upon by the expert seeking to establish with certainty the attribution of any work of sculpture? The reason, of course, is that here lies something comparable with handwriting characteristics or the skin ridges of the finger ends employed in the finger-print identification method of humans. It is a higher level parallel giving outward expression to basic matters of originality; using the word not with the emphasis on innovation but with the emphasis on individuality, uniqueness. This concept of individuality is one that seems to be particularly developed as a characteristic of our civilization as it evolved through the Classical, the Renaissance to the Occidental. It is an attitude of looking to each individual to make a unique contribution to the cultural sum possessed by mankind. Each artist worthy to be called an individual will give something to mankind which no one else born, or to be born can, or ever will be able to give. It is a more important aspect of the activity of artistic creation than that of being an innovator, in the sense of being the starter of a new phase of fashion. Although this is the aspect more commonly equated with the word originality. But the passing of time, bringing as it does the fluctuations of fashion, makes this aspect relatively unimportant in the long view. However, originality in the former sense can be, and often is, concurrent with being the innovator of a new movement, but this is a less important side effect, which often takes place.

It is to be in a vulnerable position not fully to understand the nature of the principles on which the structure of opinion opposite to one's own is founded. The extreme case of the opposite view to the one put forward in this book is that the élite artist is a kind of widely operating designer. He is a designer only and quite remote from all the processes of manipulating materials, which aspect of the creation of a work of art is relegated to the province of the skilled artisan for execution. It is necessary that these artisans should have skill without ideas. Any individuality or initiative that they might display obviously must be, in these circumstances, an intrusion between the designer-artist and the perfect realization of his intention. Men are needed in this process, as machines sufficiently versatile to meet the circumstances are inconceivable. But what is essential to this approach for it to operate perfectly is a pool of highly skilled men

4

2. Mark Batten. *Figure of Founder, Trinity College, Oxford.* Over life-size in Clipsham stone

without the disruptive quality of ideas of their own. Some kind of controlling link between the completely non-manual designer and the actual maker of the work of art is a requisite of this method. Such processes do exist and much ingenuity has been put into their invention. The purist form of this approach to the creation of a work of art is exemplified in the operation of an architect in relation to builders. There are sculptors who operate in a similar way. The success or failure of this method is manifestly dependent on the possibility or the impossibility of creating this link. Can it be of perfect efficiency? The theme of this book is that the field of the fine arts is one giving a unique sort of opportunity to mankind. In this field a work, such as a sculpture, is bound to fall far short of the possibilities open to it if this remote control and impersonal guidance procedure is used for its production. It is necessary for the artist to be involved in the most intimate manner attainable in all aspects of the process of creation of the work of art. Only in this way can the intense quality of communication that is possible, be realized. Nothing less is good enough for the fine arts.

This view of regarding an artist as a widely ranging designer not involved in the actual processes of manipulating materials, looking upon it only from a remote and theoretical standpoint, gives us the group of artists not especially tied to any particular material and technique. It is one point of view; the opposite to the point of view advocated in this book. It has its advantages. For instance, it is well adapted to the creation of very large works which can hardly be made by the methods recommended here. I am thinking of works of the size of the Mount Rushmore Sculptures, or the Statue of Liberty in the U.S.A. or the sculptures on the Arc de Triumph or the Henry Moore figure outside the U.N.E.S.C.O. Headquarters in Paris. While the making of works of this size is scarcely possible by the method of direct carving in stone does not consideration of these examples, in fact, demonstrate my point?

With, possibly, the exception of the, now much battered, Great Sphinx in Egypt, of mysterious origin, these huge works fulfill a useful function for society but they do not at the same time really come into the category of the fine arts at all, by fulfilling the very special function performed by this branch of human activity.

This non-executant widely ranging designer type of artist certainly tends, in our civilization, to attract to himself higher prestige by becoming equated with the directors of affairs in the sphere of politics and business. On the other hand the directly material-manipulating

6

type of artist tends to become equated with workmen with their understandably lower prestige rating. I say, understandably, because in contemporary industry the workman has in fact lower skill. It is impercipient to take this view of the artist, the authentic type, who creates his work by means of the exploitation of the existing processes of an established handicraft by transmuting its techniques for the superior purposes of fine art. Furthermore, the non-executant-designer type of artist assessed by fundamental standards is himself revealed as being intrinsically no more than a kind of drawing board operative, or perhaps if more successful professionally, a director of the activities of draughtsmen in a drawing office. In the field of sculpture itself the corresponding method of approach makes what is commonly called the master sculptor, in practice and in fact, merely a maker of maquettes (small scale models of clay, or wax) and a supervisory director of artisans. It is the theme of this book to show that this kind of relationship between the artist and the actual work is of a character far too remote and giving a mode of control much too devious to accomplish the kind of results demanded in the special sphere of the fine arts although it is adequate for the less demanding general activities of mankind. The practice and the advocacy of this view of the artist as a non-executant designer is based on the concept of an abrupt separation in consciousness between the faculty of generating ideas and the other facilities and thus regarding it as an activity existing in a state of isolation, remote from the manual operations involved in the creation of the work of art. The cleavage of specialization made here between an activity envisaged as ideas propagation in vacuity without preferential inclination to particular materials and techniques, and the other zones of consciousness, such as that of the choice and manipulation of materials, is to try to establish the concept of specialization at quite the wrong point. From this mistaken way of thinking stems the fallacious view of the artist without temperamentally inspired preferences in the field of material and technique because he is falsely conceived of as altogether withdrawn from this sphere. These are not the conditions within which great works of art can be created.

Specialization does come in and potently, but in quite another way. In fact, conversely, it is connected with the intense involvement of the artist in matters of material and technique as an essential part of the conditions required for that maximum degree of communication of which nothing less will suffice for the fine arts. This is not overlooking the fact that sculptors commonly do other kinds of work, for instance, drawing. But their drawings stand in a contributory relationship to their sculpture. While the sculpture is at the focal point of their system of communication the drawings gain their validity in the main from displaying in their every quality their contributory relationship to sculpture. Actually looking at sculptors' drawings makes this point more clearly than exposition can do.

It is evident that any artist of serious purpose and above all a sculptor must become intensely involved in specialization in the field of material and technique. From this a two-pronged quest emerges for the sculptor. Firstly, in what group of material and technique can his personal vision find fulfilment within the governing influence of his congenital temperament. Secondly, what are the comparative merits of the various existing or potential materials and techniques in their own right and independently of his subjective response to them. This must be a powerfully preponderating factor of choice because some material and technique groups manifestly have an intrinsic superiority for aesthetic or practical reasons although individual sculptors may not personally find themselves able fully to respond to them. Nevertheless, such superiority where it exists must obviously be taken into account.

It will have been noticed that in many places in the text the terms material and techniques are linked as a duality and this intended reiteration is to emphasize the importance of holding this fact in mind in thinking about sculpture. Whereas in the field of painting and the allied field of constructiveism, for any one material, a much wider latitude of technique potential exists than is the case with sculpture. In other words, in sculpture the chosen material dictates the technique in a more restrictive manner. And to attempt to evade or ignore this is to lapse into capriciousness.

To return to the examination of questions of material and technique, as has already been said, the personal response of the individual sculptor to any one is a particular matter of his own concern. The general enquiry, to be pursued here, is to compare the intrinsic merits, for purposes of sculpture, of the materials which nature provides and also those that are sometimes called man-made. It is often overlooked that, strictly speaking, there can be no such thing as man-made materials. For basically all raw materials come in some form from nature. Those that are commonly called man-made are, in fact, the ones whose more complex processing has brought about changes which make them unrecognizable as the products of their natural source to ordinary

8

casual observation: and at the same time their properties have been much changed.

What are the qualities required of a material to make it rank high among those suitable for sculpture?

Foremost, the material for sculpture must be hard and enduring. Most sculpture will be called upon to stand out of doors some of the time and hence all sculpture material, intended as it may be either for indoors or out, should for safety, be capable of withstanding the weather. Although the material must be hard, strong and durable it must, of course, be possible to shape it by some means not intolerably arduous or time-consuming. Unfortunately, it is in the nature of life, in a general sort of way, that the materials which are the most durable are also the hardest and most difficult to work. The phrase above, in a general sort of way, allows for a certain measure of exception to this rule. This exceptional trend, where it occurs, will be compared later but is, even so, a matter of drawing a balance between degrees of advantage on one side or the other.

Secondly, and obviously, the appearance of the material must be good. Here again, in the course of their evaluation for sculpture purposes, a balance has to be drawn between the various advantages of potential materials. Some materials have self colour, which will be permanent and is in itself beautiful and is also of a character suitable for a wide range of sculptural ideas. Other potential materials are in themselves negative for colour but can be coloured, each with a degree of permanence which varies.

Thirdly, and closely linked with colour, is surface texture. Some materials can be polished, or some may come up to a smooth shiny surface in other kinds of finishing processes. Other materials have an inescapably granular or other kind of rough surface which will be suitable for a limited range of ideas.

Fourthly, the method of working demanded by certain materials imparts a characteristic surface texture to the sculpture in an automatic kind of way. This is one of the predominant generators of surface texture and covers a very wide range. To illustrate with but two examples, the operation of the flame of the blow-torch, in oxyacetylene welding and cutting steel for sculpture, can produce a 'frozen' ripple texture in some parts of the work and in others, various kinds of intentional raggedness. Whereas the process of grinding down to the finished shape, of stones of some very hard kinds, produces a smooth suave texture. And, by contrast, finishing some

9

less hard kinds of stone, with a claw tool, imparts another characteristic texture, in this case, a rough one.

Fifthly, to turn away from consideration of the appearance of the material, there remains to be assessed, one of the most important aspects of all. This is the one quality that must be possessed by any potential material for sculpture. The nature of the material must permit the process of making the actual shape of the sculpture to be completely under the control of the sculptor himself, without the intervention of elaborate machinery, or of teams of workmen. Furthermore, its properties must be such that the development of the greatest possible refinement of shape and also many subtle readjustments of shape, can be carried out by the sculptor's own hand unimpeded. And it must be possible to make these throughout a long period. The process of shaping the material must therefore be able to be based on human manual skill alone. This, of course, includes tools, which may be power driven. But a nice distinction must here be drawn between power driven tools and machines. In this context a tool, whether power driven or not, is a thing fully guided by manual skill, whereas a machine is a thing merely adjusted and then set in motion by hand, to carry out the operation automatically.

Once the sculptor has fixed the final shape, from that point on, it is not inconsistent for elaborate and indirect processes to be brought into play and in the case of some groups of sculpture materials this takes place of necessity. For instance, sculptures in metals such as bronze or aluminium are made by casting in a mould which is made from the sculptor's clay model by a chain of processes. The metal is melted by great heat and poured into the mould, where it cools and solidifies to become the final form of the sculpture. This chain of processes is very rarely carried out by the sculptor himself nowadays. It is done by specializing plaster casters and bronze founders. Then again, for some types of sculpture in plastics, the sculptor will, similarly, establish the final shape in the form of a clay model. Thereafter, a chain of processes of another kind takes place, to bring the actual sculpture into being in the plastic material. The point of note is that these and other similar processes, however complicated and intricate, take place after the shape of the sculpture has been brought to finality in the clay model. This is not, therefore, inconsistent with the conditions set out above.

From all the different kinds of matter which the world presents, sculptors have made a selection for their particular purpose. And, being endowed with the properties already stated as necessary,

10

3. MARK BATTEN. *The Diogenist.* Life-size figure in Hopton-wood stone

there are set out below, in the form of a list, the main groups of materials that have been found suitable for sculpture. Of this list, some materials fulfil the conditions very well and some less well, but adequately.

1   Stones, of many kinds.
2   Metals, of many kinds.
3   Concrete and similar substances; based on hydraulic cements such as Portland or Ciment Fondu.
4   Terracotta.
5   Plastic mixtures, of several kinds.
6   Ivory and Bone.
7   Woods, of many kinds.
8   Glass.
9   Combinations of two or more of the above.

Applied science is constantly engaged in research with the object of discovering new hard and durable materials for use in building, manufacture and engineering. Sculptors are on the watch to give any of these materials that are produced an experimental try-out in their field. While, of course, not having been produced with sculpture in mind, there is, nevertheless, always the possibility that one of these materials will turn out to be suitable for sculpture. However, it is more of a possibility than a probability, because the properties required of a sculpture material are out of the range of those demanded by building or industry or engineering in one respect. Thus, in industry a paramount need is adaptability to mass production of huge numbers of exact replicas while massiveness and complexity of the apparatus to process the material into shape is not a serious drawback. The exact opposite in this respect are the qualities needed of a material for it to be suitable for the sculptor's purpose. So it is that only by a fortunate chance will one of these new materials developed for industry by applied science be of use to the sculptor. Nevertheless this has happened in one or two cases.

A gushingly forward-looking attitude of mind to the search for good material for sculpture should be restrained by reflection on the fact that the motor car and much else of today is manufactured mainly of the same material, steel, that was used to make the weapons of the Roman soldiers of two thousand years ago. Thus we find also in the field of sculpture that the traditional materials are not supplanted by new ones. They are only supplemented by them. The traditional materials are seen, on balance, to retain many elements of superiority. The main advantage, often the only advantage, of the new materials

12

is in the field of cheapness. This takes two forms. The material may be actually cheaper to buy. Secondly, in most cases, it is much quicker to work and this leads to cost advantage. On the other side of the balance such new materials as have yet appeared are greatly inferior in appearance and durability.

It is paradoxical that in so many cases sculptors, seeming to give support to the newer materials by their employment of them, at the same time try to make them imitate the appearance of the traditional ones. In this they are, in fact, unwittingly giving support to the view that the traditional ones are superior. And we shall see that it is not because of a conservative outlook, that for sculpture, the traditional materials are preferred by both the majority of sculptors and the majority of connoisseurs. It is for the best reasons in both the aesthetic and the practical fields, as will become evident as the book proceeds.

An epitome of the methods of working the various materials for sculpture, which have been listed above, is called for at this point.

The different kinds of stone cover a wide range of hardness and texture but the methods of working them may, in general, be called carving. At the softer end of the scale, stone can be sawn with a frame saw for discardable blades. In the hardest ranges, finishing can only be done by grinding, with something like Carborundum, or abrasive hones made of industrial diamond chips. Between these extremes, kinds of stone are carved with hammer and chisel or punch action.

Metals are worked in two different ways. In one, a very indirect way, a mould is made and the metal is melted by great heat and poured in liquid form into it. Here, it takes the shape of the mould, cools and resumes its hard state and the mould is then removed, leaving the metal sculpture as the end product. The shape of the sculpture has been previously fixed by making a model in some soft material, like clay or wax. The mould has to be made from this clay model by an intermediate casting process employing plaster of paris. This is a highly summary description of a most complicated and indirect process. The other way of making sculpture in metal is the direct way, the constructional way. The key tool in this method is the oxy-acetylene blow-torch fed by cylinders of compressed gas. The, quite small, flame of this is so hot that it will quickly melt any metal, even steel. This melting power is used for two different purposes, by adjustment of the flame and the manner in which it is handled. The flame can be made, either, to cut apart, or to join together pieces of metal; cutting, or welding. Thus, this kind of metal sculpture is directly constructed by a technique exploiting all the variations which this allows. Non-ferrous metals, such as bronze or aluminium, are the ones mainly used in the first method. In the second method steel is the most commonly used metal.

In the case of concrete and similar substances a parallelism with the above occurs, with a division into two channels of technique. In the one, concrete, in liquid form, is poured into a mould, in which it sets hard in time, in about a week. In the same sort of way as for metal the mould is made from a clay model and the whole process is a chain of stages very similar to those followed for casting sculpture in metal. This is the indirect technique branch. Also in this group of materials there is the opportunity for a direct constructional technique process. For this method an armature (a metal frame) is made, for the start, and a mixture, based on a quick setting hydraulic cement, is made in a series of batches. This mixture, as well as being quick setting, is made up with a stiffer consistency than concrete for pouring. This mixture is smeared on to the armature with large spatulas and allowed the right time to get stiff enough to support further layers. By continuing this process of adding layer upon layer the sculpture is gradually built up. The slow setting hydraulic cement, for the concrete, is called Portland and the quick setting hydraulic cement, for the direct technique, is called Ciment Fondu.

For terracotta a convenient natural fact is exploited. This is, that the sculpture can be modelled in a suitable sort of clay. This actual clay model can then be dried slowly and when dry, can be heated in a special kind of furnace, called a kiln. This is kept at a temperature in the region of red hot for the correct length of time. In this way the soft clay becomes transformed into hard pottery, or like a building brick. Essentially, this is in fact the same process as pottery making, or brick making. And, furthermore, clay, almost in its natural state, is, in any case, the best and most commonly used material for modelling. So this natural fact is very convenient for those sculptors who find in modelling for terracotta a sympathetic technique.

The materials called plastics are employed in sculpture making in two ways. Plastic materials, of the one kind, themselves form the whole bulk of the sculpture. The material is made to change its condition from a soft pliable state to a hard state. In the case of the other way of using them, different kinds of plastic are made to form a matrix, or cement, to other materials which make up the main bulk. The change from the soft to the hard state is brought about, mainly, in one of two ways. Plastics of the one group become hard on exposure

14

to the air. Those of the other group are made to harden by the addition of another chemical. Materials used to reinforce, or to make up the bulk where plastics are acting only as a cement, are usually metal of some kind, in a powdered or a granulated state, with fibre-glass reinforcement. Fibre-glass is glass spun into thin threads. These threads are formed into a sort of cloth or felt which is flexible.

The technique for making the sculptures follows ways similar to those employed in the cases of both metals and of concrete and similarly offers two main alternatives of an indirect and a direct technique. Plastic sculpture is either cast in a mould, which has been prepared from a clay model, during which stage the shape is worked out. Alternatively, it is built up in a direct way, by a constructional method, in successive layers, with a spatula, and the shape is thus worked out on the final object, the actual sculpture itself.

Ivory or bone is made use of as a sculpture material by carving methods. Both can be sawn, drilled, with a rotating drill, pared, with a knife-like tool, rasped, and polished with fine abrasives. From the point of view of the actual making process, there is with these materials no alternative, to working in a direct way.

Wood, as with ivory, can only be made into sculpture by the carving technique, which, from the working point of view, is a direct method, to which there is no alternative. It can be sawn, drilled with a rotating drill, rasped, smoothed with abrasives and polished with waxes. But it lends itself especially to being worked with a mallet and sharp edged chisels and gouges. Wood sculpture can be made of separate pieces joined together, which has been done in the past and is done at present, to some extent. In the past it was often coated with gesso and painted.

Glass, as a sculpture material, can be worked in two alternative ways. It can be melted and cast in a mould (indirect), or it can be carved, to a limited extent, with rotating grinding wheels, whose cutting surfaces are furnished with industrial diamonds, (direct). Up to the present its application to sculpture has been of limited scope. However, it should be noted, that in its fibre-glass form, it is one of the most important of the materials added to plastic, as a reinforcement or a bulk producer, in creating sculpture in plastic.

Of the materials briefly described above the traditional ones are the following five: stones, metals, terracotta, ivory or bone, woods. These alone therefore, are the ones whose behaviour under the passage of time, time reckoned in hundreds, or even thousands of years, is a matter of experience. Thus their comparative durability, and theirs alone, is a thoroughly known factor meriting the utmost confidence. Although scarcely to be counted a traditional sculpture material, glass may be added, as a substance whose durability is very well known by experience in comparison with others.

Laboratory tests of sculpture materials give useful information in a short time, but it has been shown that they cannot give a verdict of finality. In the weathering of materials, under the passage of time, influences operate in ways not reproducable within laboratory test conditions. Even in the relatively short time that laboratory tests have been available for comparison, it has been notable that their indications have not been always in accord with factual information, gained from practical experience.

Of the sculpture materials, for which we have the evidence derived from the experience of thousands of years, two have shown themselves the most outstandingly durable and these are stone, of certain kinds, and castings of the metal bronze, (bronze is not a single metal but is an alloy, or 'mixture', of copper and tin). Stone and bronze are unquestionably an outstanding pair by comparison with the other materials, but to draw a balance between these two brings in complicated factors. During periods when certain sculptures have been neglected and have become buried under earth and the rubble of ruins for hundreds of years, stone has usually resisted distinctly the better of the two and has eventually come out in better relative condition. For the stone of sculpture, neglected and underground, has the advantage that it is in its normal habitat, in which, as a raw material, it had formerly spent millions of years. On the other hand, it must, in scientific impartiality be admitted, that in other conditions occurring during the last hundred years, which has been a period of severe atmospheric pollution in industrialized countries, bronze sculpture has resisted better than some stone in industrial cities in Northern climates. But atmospheric pollution may well now be declining, even in industrial districts and is, furthermore, as an ordeal for stone, confined to these limited regions.

If all sculptures spent only a pampered existence in air-conditioned art museums the question of the durability of their material would scarcely arise. But two factors of a totally different kind, each in its own way, makes the strength and durability of the material of paramount importance. The first, a simple straightforward one, is the practical fact that a large proportion of sculpture has an architectural function and usually has to be permanently out of doors, exposed to the weather.

The second factor does not stem directly from physical and chemical influences. It is instead the outcome of certain mental characteristics of the race of mankind itself. The course of history reveals that mankind behaves according to a rhythm in time which is variously called the fluctuations of trends, or the changes of fashion, or of the vogue. This is a deeper matter, having more important influences, than it is commonly taken to be. It shows itself to be very deep seated and to be irresistible, except by a small minority of individuals and to be mainly an unconscious thing; unconscious in the way that it is not recognized for what it is. While this trait is a permanent characteristic of mankind, it was for our own age to elevate it, in a slightly new form, to be set up as a chief article of faith and one not ever to be submitted to critical examination. In our age each movement in this rhythmic series, not recognized for what it really is, is thought of as being the operation of a mysterious process of progress, which is envisaged as a course of perpetual, universal and inevitable improvement, taking place during the passage of time. It is taken as a constant movement undeviatingly in one direction, metaphorically, upwards. This attitude makes people of our period even more calculatedly ruthless in rejecting the works of art of any immediately preceding phase.

While being at least as bigoted in this respect as the people of previous periods of history the art community of today is organized in a more integrated and comprehensive way. Also the tempo of all changes of direction of trends is accelerated. Thus, considering the question of the survival of any work of art there is a period of maximum danger for it, which is certainly no less in our age than in the past. This critical period of maximum danger of non-survival for a work of art is the phase immediately following the one in which it was created; created as it must have been, at least to some extent, in conformity with the currently accepted climate of aesthetic opinion. Briefly, in other words, the period in which it is considered old fashioned, without having yet become old enough to be accepted as an antique. History shows that a work of art is never, even if it survives a thousand years or more, held in such low esteem as it is in this relatively brief period. For it is in this way that human behaviour in the field of fashion, or the vogue, operates.

This is not a philosophical digression irrelevant to the subject under consideration, namely, the comparison of the relative durability of stone and bronze sculpture. Because this factor of human behaviour has as powerful a bearing on the matter, in actual practice, as any of

17

the others at which we have been looking. It comes into the relative evaluation in the following way. Stone, already made into sculpture, has, for the most obvious practical reasons, almost no attraction as a re-usable raw material for any purpose. In other words it has almost no 'scrap' value. By contrast, the bronze in bronze sculpture has a very high value as a re-usable raw material and with scarcely any extra labour involved in conversion. This factor, far from being, as one might easily and wrongly suppose, of no great influence, has had a decisive influence in practice, well beyond what might be expected. Furthermore, it continues to do so. Even today, when materials are in most plentiful supply, bronze sculptures, as soon as they become unfashionable in style, are sold to be broken up for the scrap value of the bronze. And, also they are frequently stolen, in cases where they stand in positions more or less exposed to the public, to suffer the same fate.

Just one example may be taken from the distant past to illustrate the long history behind this lower survival-expectation of bronze, as a material for sculpture, compared with stone. There is plenty of unquestionable historical evidence that in Classical Greece, by, at least, the fourth century B.C. and the periods following, almost as much of the sculpture was made in bronze as was made in marble. Yet surviving bronze sculptures of this age are very rare by comparison with the relatively large number of marble sculptures which we have in our museums and private collections. Furthermore, there are a number of examples of the existence of contemporary historical descriptions of bronze sculptures of exceptional fame in their own time. They have vanished and we know them today only through the still surviving Hellenistic, or Roman, marble, *note* marble, copies made in ancient times while the bronzes still existed. There are quite a number of these in the world's museums today, which the reader can discover for himself. How did it come about that all these bronze sculptures have disappeared? They were melted down, at the orders of the soldier-raiders from Northern Europe, at the fall of the Roman Empire. Bronze sculpture was not as fashionable with them, as were bronze weapons, bronze armour and bronze cooking pots, into which they were easily converted.

The few bronze sculptures that have survived from this age have done so by fortunate accidents. For instance, they sank with ships, recovered in modern times, or were dropped into the mud of ancient harbours, and since recovered. This usually happened while they were being looted from Ancient Greece by the Romans. Lying buried

18

in sand, or mud and under water is one form of conditions within which the bronze of sculpture has lasted well.

Returning to consideration of the evaluation of stone as sculpture material from the physical standpoint here again it can be seen to be pre-eminent in another way. Stone has the decisive advantage of being intrinsically extremely strong with a range varying between the hardest granites and gabbros to the relatively softer limestones. At the top of the range, to take one of the strongest granites for example, we get the fact that a cube of only one foot size has a resistance to crushing equivalent to more than two thousand tons (the weight of a fair sized ship). That stone sculptures are necessarily always solid must be added to this in comparing the material with other kinds of sculpture materials which mostly can only be used in a hollow form. This hollow use takes the form of a very thin shell in the case of bronze and most other metal castings. It is still a hollow shell but somewhat less thin in the cases of terracotta, plastic mouldings, built-up cement constructions, etc. But against this must be reckoned the fact that these materials are either less strong or very much less strong in themselves than are metals such as bronze, so that there is no comparative gain here. In this kind of context a material like plaster of paris does not even merit consideration. As for wood, the hardest kinds, have slight to moderate strength. But it might well be noted in passing that it is not in this quarter that the most serious disadvantages of wood are to be found. These lie in its marked vulnerability to destruction by fungal rot and the ravages of boring insects such as the furniture beetle, the death-watch beetle and the powder-post beetle.

Taking all the various factors and influences, to which sculptures are exposed, into consideration, the following evaluation is established.

Sculptures in kinds of stone in the groups quartzites, grit-stones (hard, pure sandstones, auto-compacted), granites and basalts, undoubtedly outlast bronze and all other sculpture materials.

Sculptures in good quality limestones and in metamorphic lime-stones, such as marble, in most cases outlast sculptures in bronze and all other materials. Bronze, in its turn, providing it survives the melting down hazard, which is a serious one, outlasts the less good limestones, softer, impure, sandstones and stones of the serpentine, steatite, and alabaster groups.

Stone, thus seen to be, on balance, the most durable of all sculpture materials has, in addition, great advantage in the field of appearance. Stone, in all periods of history and including the present, has been recognized to have a very attractive desirable appearance; to have beauty, if one may venture to use the word in this age. Examples in support of this could be quoted from all eras, but to consider only two, take the following. Evidence of this regard for the beautiful appearance of stone is manifested, particularly, in buildings of Classical Greece and Ancient Rome, in which arrangements of different kinds of marbles and other stones formed a most important element in their decoration. To move to our own period, it is to be seen that often the only attempt which is made to relieve the utilitarian austerity of appearance of modern buildings is based on the beauty of marble and other stones, employed in the form of sawn and polished slabs, as cladding, at points where emphasis, or a focus of attention is called for. And it should be noted in this context that it is not thought necessary to bring in shape at all. Manifestly, it is felt that complete reliance can be placed on the beauty of the stone itself, used merely as a flat surface.

Stone can provide the sculptor with a quite unparalleled variety of appearance, in colour, in texture and in patterns of colours and textures. The range may be indicated, but no more than indicated, by the following few examples. We may start with black granite and black marble. These give a dense black, polished, or at choice, a matt surface. Coloured marbles are to be had in plain colours, or variegated arrangements. The colour range includes, taken as some examples only, dark green, dark red, light green shades, pink shades, blue shades, yellow shades and a great variety of brown, fawn and off-white shades, plus white itself. All of these can be used either matt, or polished, giving different effects. Other different ways of finishing the stone can give quite different appearances, if desired, between one part and another, of the same stone.

In the different kinds of stone there is available to the sculptor a further variety of choice to be found in the field of the intrinsic texture of the stone. Some stones have a close dense texture, like metal and some, a coarsely porous and open one and there are all the degrees between. In this connection fossils in stone may be considered. These have a slightly different constitution from the matrix of the stone in which they are embedded. They exist in many varieties of stone and in all sizes, up to very large size; and also in a highly recognizable form, or less so. In the past they have been hated by sculptors as troublesome chance occurrences. But I feel that in the present climate of aesthetic opinion they could be exploited in a manner considered interesting, having affinity with the *objet trouvé*

4. MARK BATTEN. *Mermaid*. In off-white coloured Craigleith stone from the quarry near Edinburgh, and dark green marble from one of the quarries on the Greek island of Tino (see pages 119 and 122). This is an example of the employment, referred to in the text, of different kinds of stone jointed together; in this case by a mortise and tenon joint, carved in the stone. As an easier method, a cramp, or a bolt for a makeshift, and cement mixture may be used; but if a cramp is used it must be of bronze, not steel

movement, in contemporary art, by those people in sympathy with this movement. It should be noted, in passing, that certain kinds of stone are totally composed of an agglomeration of small fossils. The kinds of stone with a dense, close texture can, at will, be brought, either, to a slight degree of polish, (usually called egg-shell), or to a very high degree of polish, like glass. The range of less dense textured stones can be brought up only to the egg-shell polish. It may be taken as a general rule that, when polished, the colour of stones becomes considerably darker in tone and stronger in shade, than they take on with the matt surface. This provides additional alternatives at the choice of the sculptor using stone.

Stone possesses another advantage in the field of appearance. This is that sculptures in stone have a distinctive quality somewhat elusive of description but, nonetheless, very real. They possess what may be described as a presence. Some of the more obvious reasons for this, are that they proclaim, even to the most cursory examination, that they are neither hollow nor flimsy. And furthermore, it is very obvious that the substance of them is genuine, solid, all-through stuff, in contrast to coatings and veneers. This is even more telling in our period, characteristically, one of increasing resort to thin layers and platings of high grade materials, fixed over bases of coarse, inferior, materials.

The processes of carving stone impose on the sculptor a certain discipline which is disadvantageous only from the grossest commercial point of view; in regard, that is, to the amount of time consumed. From the point of view of aesthetics this commercial disadvantage is of no relevance. Rather is this time consuming nature of the work beneficial at an important level, in that it forces the work to go at a pace more conducive to taking deep thought and making only well considered moves. The hardness of the stone, occasioning as it does, powerful and an evenly distributed resistance to manipulation of the surface, tends to curb random, near-accidental, or ill-considered variations of the form. This is positive in its influence on an effort to generate forms of a suave, lucid, sublime character. Furthermore, this physical resistance of the stone and the feelings engendered by its essential nature discourage, in particular, inappropriate incursive developments in the design. Additionally beneficial aesthetically, as it will be seen, is the sheer muscle work involved in the rather laborious process of carving stone. This idea is not expected to commend itself to the disciples of 'get it quick and easy'; it is, nonetheless, true. The fact that a thing akin to the pleasure of

22

bodily activity enjoyed through sport and athletics takes place also in stone carving is transmitted to the sculpture and thereby conveyed to the viewer. A convexity here and a hollow there, the tool marks of the surface textures showing the kind of tools employed and the scale of the pattern, the power of the strokes that produced them, is but one example of the way in which this comes about.

To return to a theme touched upon earlier, in the outline summary of the various ways of working sculpture materials, it is appropriate at this point to take the examination of it a stage further.

The term 'direct sculpture' has a kind of two level interpretation. In one, 'direct sculpture' is taken to mean no more than that the actual object which the viewer sees, the sculpture, is the very one in which the shape has been worked out and fixed. To clarify this it is necessary to example the opposite procedure, in which the sculptor carries out all the work on and fixes the shape in, for instance, a clay model. This clay model forms only the prototype from which an object is made by indirect and elaborate processes in an altogether different material. This secondary, end-product, object is, in this case, the actual sculpture that the viewer sees; the prototype being discarded. Under this first interpretation of the term, all sculpture in stone is necessarily to be considered 'direct sculpture' and within this classification should be included also those in wood, ivory and constructional sculpture in welded steel and other metals, built-up concrete, built-up plastic and built-up terracotta sculpture.

The second interpretation of the term 'direct sculpture', if we add—'in stone', is, it will be noticed, the title of this book and is a more restricted and purist interpretation of the term. As was pointed out above, by the first interpretation all sculpture in stone is 'direct sculpture'. But only some of stone sculpture is 'direct' by this second meaning given to the term. Thus some of stone sculpture is indirect, according to this classification, because it has not been actually carved by the sculptor with his own hands. It has been carved by artisans, using mechanical copying methods, from a prototype prepared by the sculptor, by modelling in clay. It is often totally untouched by the so-called sculptor himself. Furthermore and worse still, he, in many cases, cannot himself even carve stone at all and knows little about it. Another, and somewhat different procedure, also comes within this classification, as not direct. In this, the sculptor first works out to completion a clay model of the sculpture. From this he makes a plaster cast and then sets out, himself, to copy his own modelling into stone, by measuring his own work, by the elaborate mechanical method called pointing!

The historical background of these matters and a more detailed assessment will be found to follow later in the book.

With no thought of disparaging in any way the many great works that have undoubtedly been created in other materials, most sculptors have, at the back of their minds the view that, generally speaking, the direct carvers in stone constitute an élite within the art. Unintentional support for this view has often been given by artists with a brilliant talent for modelling but with, at the same time, no feeling for stone who have, nevertheless, felt a compulsion to embark upon stone carving and with unhappy results. After all, the very name 'sculptor' means carver, derived as it is from the Latin *sculpere*, to carve. Thus it is a sort of courtesy title to give the name of sculptor to those who produce their work by modelling in clay. In Renaissance times when those who produced figures and heads in bronze first came to be called sculptors it was not so inappropriate a designation; because their work was deliberately modelled and cast with an allowance for finishing. The final form was created by a process of chiselling and riffling. Thus they were in fact largely carvings in bronze, the modelling and casting being looked upon as preliminary stages of the work. No one in those times thought of exhibiting as finished work a cast in straight-from-the-mould state as they usually now do. (This must be taken in a relative sense because there is obviously a minimum amount of work which must be done to a bronze cast before it can be shown.)

I turn now more closely to the theme of my book, the explanation of the making of sculptures from stone by the direct carving technique; a technique which we know to have been almost unchanged for at least five thousand years. A technique, moreover, which continues the same for exceedingly good reasons, both practical and aesthetic; it is both old, and in its revival, very new.

It will be realized that to be engrossed in such an ageless calling cannot fail to reduce somewhat one's sense of kinship of mind with people, on the opposite hand, who are mainly pre-occupied with things that have only been going on during the present decade. Such people are like enough to find the mental alignment of stone carvers a little strange; it may be looked upon as an occupational idiosyncrasy holding sway over the minds of this community, the stone carvers. It springs from experiences of such a kind as placing one's own carvings, or actually working them on the fabric of ancient buildings. The stone under one's own hand and tool is here to be

24

5. MARK BATTEN. *John Hull Grundy Esq*. Portrait bust made by the direct carving technique; it is sometimes claimed that a disadvantage of the direct carving technique is that portraits cannot be done by this method. (Courtesy Mrs. A. Hull Grundy)

seen touching that other stone imprinted with the tool strokes which are an echo of the motions of the hands of some stone carver of hundreds of years ago. Such an experience evokes emotional and mental responses under the impact of which the sense of time dissolves and one levitates into a state of consciousness in which this bygone stone carver is felt to be more one's fellow than, for an example, the man at the garage today. It can be an equally moving experience to study the tool traces on, perhaps, a Greek sculpture of five hundred years B.C., or an Egyptian one many thousands of years old. One realizes that one has oneself made such tool marks only yesterday. So is the routine of a sculptor's life made up, centred as it must be on the idea of progress towards better work, a life, therefore, which cannot but involve much study of antique sculpture. It should be realized that progressing towards to an improved understanding of some ancient sculpture's qualities may, in fact, be quite as 'progressive' as trying to be a sort of soothsayer and foresee future trends. This does not mean that a stone carver has less interest in things purely contemporary, but he does tend, as one outcome of his very absorbing work, to see them in a different perspective from people in many other occupations. For example, the author's consuming preoccupation with stone carving did not actually prevent him from becoming, during the war, a quite efficient instructor in the driving and maintenance of Armoured Fighting Vehicles, in the Household Cavalry. Probably it did make him a rather abstracted and, from the military point of view, tiresome one.

Sculpture, and pre-eminently stone sculpture, has one property which makes it unique among all the products of the mind and hand of man. Nothing survives having comparable power of vivid and intimate communication to us of the ideas of long past civilizations. It is the least blurred voice from the past; and the only one from the civilizations of very remote antiquity. Folk-lore, myths and legends are probably those things which most approach stone sculpture in this respect; but it is very obvious how exposed they are to being corrupted in the purity of their record by the constant pressure, through the passing ages, of moulding influences. In the case of inscriptions and other writings, their language has to be rediscovered by scholars which puts them in a secondary category compared with sculpture as regards intimacy of communication. By the most astounding contrast to all else a sculpture of, say, five thousand years ago is unearthed and at once one sees straight into the mind of a man of antiquity: contemplating its toolwork one can feel in one's own

26

6. After the passage of two hundred million years these fossilised foot prints of a prehistoric creature remain an immediate record of the movements of its body (Courtesy British Museum, Natural History Section)

flesh the echoes of the very gestures of his hands with an unparalleled intimacy. As the fossilized footprints of some prehistoric beast of many millions of years ago are a perpetual record of the movements of its vanished flesh, so the tooling on a sculpture thousands of years old is a sort of fossilization of the movements of the sculptor.

There is greater analogy between sculpture and fossils than would at first appear. They are made of the same material, stone, and if they spend likewise long quiescent periods underground they have, potentially, the same power to endure for millions of years.

Of course not everyone can appreciate sculpture and not every type of idea is capable of being thus fossilized and preserved in perpetuity. Even so, sculpture has the role of forming the main link between the civilizations that rise and fall as time unfolds.

This leads me to another point. Some pedantically-minded historians and archaeologists have claimed that the kind of ideas that we nowadays call aesthetic had no part in the creation of ancient

7. Similarly, after more than two thousand years these toolmarks endure as an intimate record of the movements of an individual sculptor's hands, as if fossilised into stone (Courtesy British Museum)

8. Comparable toolmarks recording the movements of the hands of the author in the present time, a record of movement in, as it were, fossil form

sculpture. They must base this contention mainly on the non-existence of writing about aesthetics; or none that has been discovered or deciphered. The indecisiveness of this evidence is obvious. We know of no ancient civilization that indulged in the flood of writing which is a characteristic of ours. In any case, I wonder if archaeologists of the next era, excavating on the site of the ruins of London or New York, would find any carved inscriptions on the subject of aesthetics. It is not the kind of matter that goes into such things. I am convinced that the actual qualities exhibited by the sculptures themselves are conclusive evidence that these stone carvers were actuated by urges remarkably similar to those which generate the subtleties of sculptures created today. In fact, the thing which never fails to astound me is the extraordinary feeling of familiarity and identity of outlook which one feels on seeing the work of even the earliest sculptors. They, no doubt, did as we still do; they made the more obvious aspects of their sculptures serve the purposes of their patrons and served their own purposes within the subtleties of the work.

From what has gone before it will be plain to those who know what is meant by the term 'direct carving' that for me it is unthinkable to employ any other technique for making sculpture in stone. I take the view that, while much adequate work in stone has actually been produced by the other approach it has been produced in spite of the fundamental wrongness of the method. I most strongly oppose the attitude that sculptures are merely objects made in three-dimensions; that their form is to be settled in the easiest working material, namely, clay, and that it is of little significance what material they are to be translated into to give them permanence. I believe that the material, stone, and furthermore, the particular kind of stone chosen, should in each case have an integral place in the sum of ideas which each sculpture is created to embody. Although, as I have said, adequate work has been done in the form of stone replicas of clay models none of it bears comparison with the world's greatest direct carvings.

I feel that I must here digress to ensure that I am not misunderstood. Most emphatically, I am not putting forward the claim that modelling is, as a technique, inferior to stone carving; but what I am emphasizing is that modelling should in no way be employed as *a preliminary stage* in producing a stone carving.

It is paradoxical that almost the only way to explain simply what the direct carving technique is, has to take the form of explaining what it is not. This in spite of the fact that direct carving is in reality a very positive matter. At this point I can best proceed by outlining briefly the history of the stone carving techniques.

From earliest known times until about the beginning of the eighteenth century all stone sculpture was produced by direct carving. This was so although undeniably apprentices and assistants were often employed on roughing out stages of the work. During the first part of the eighteenth century the other practice was introduced and seems rapidly to have become universal, being very well suited to the temper of the times. By the nineteenth century the traditional technique of direct carving had been lost and forgotten. By that time all sculptures in stone were merely copies, executed by skilful journeymen stone carvers, from prototypes in plaster or terracotta. The prototype from which the replica in stone was made was produced by modelling in clay or wax by the man who was, in those days, called the sculptor. This artist never touched the stone and the tradesman stone carver only copied by means of a system of measurement called 'pointing'. This system of measurement in time became ingenious and fantastically elaborate to the extent that it was common for several thousand points of measurement to be established on the prototype (a plaster cast or terracotta) and reproduced in the stone copy. The selected 'points' are marked on the prototype by the copyist and then he drills down into the block of stone with a rotating drill to the corresponding point discovered by the measurements taken. When enough of these 'points' have been established he carves away the stone where necessary as indicated by the 'points'. In this way he slowly and laboriously produces a banal copy of the plaster cast made by the artist. It could scarcely be hoped that an object produced in this way could evoke the subtle feelings, emotion and delight dwelt upon earlier in this book, the rightful concomitant of any work of art. A man can control only his own hands, not any other man's hands, with sufficient precision to execute the inspired subtleties demanded in the creation of a work of art.

It is necessary to give at least this much of a picture of what happened to sculpture in the nineteenth century to show how the tradition of direct carving had been completely lost. At the time when the late Eric Gill began the revival of direct carving, no 'artist' had carved in stone for a period of nearly two hundred years. In the year 1909 he became the first man in modern times to carve a figure directly in stone. Very soon afterwards a small group of people, including Epstein and Gaudier-Brzeska were also doing it. A fact not now generally realized is that the whole technique of direct carving

9. MARK BATTEN. *Field Marshal Smuts*. Posthumously done portrait head.
Another portrait made by the direct carving technique; as stated earlier, it is
sometimes claimed that a disadvantage of the direct carving technique is that
portraits cannot be done by this method.

had to be rediscovered by these enthusiasts. There was no one from whom to learn anything but the aforementioned journeymen copyists and the building masonry workmen. The first could teach nothing; could only corrupt. The second, the masons, had no more than the most elementary technique which was applicable only to their kind of tasks.

This revival of direct carving brought a renaissance of sculpture built on the enthusiasm of these pioneers. Unfortunately, the absence of an unbroken tradition, with the consequent complete lack, in the art world, of any knowledge of stone carving and technical matters about stone had a harmful effect and led to failures, unrecognized at the time. The principles and motives displayed could not have been more commendable. On the other hand, for the above reason, this renaissance of direct carving, in actual practice, sometimes suffered from a tinkering amateurishness which has tended to linger. Conversely, the practice and teaching of modelling has enjoyed the advantage of an unbroken tradition of 'know-how'. Matters were made worse than they need have been by the cool, or nearly hostile, attitude of the Ministry of Education Art Department to sculpture carving in stone in the years of the nineteen twenties, thirties and into the fifties. This, operating with hostility from other quarters, prevented the stone carving renaissance penetrating schools of art in Britain to any worthwhile extent. It is most surprising, after all the enthusiastic outpourings of the direct carving renaissance, to see how little real understanding of the subject penetrated schools of art. They continued to teach all students to approach sculpture solely by way of modelling, with a little tinkering with stone at the post graduate stages and as an afterthought. Before the carving of sculpture in stone could be taught properly, it was temporarily (I hope) swept into oblivion as far as art schools are concerned by the wave of the new materials and the new attitudes in art. Thus no sound professional technique of carving sculpture in stone ever came to be taught regularly in our schools of art. This has yet to come about. Would-be direct carvers, have even now, largely to find their own way through, more in spite of the so-called sculpture schools, than by help from them.

Mainly as a result of this situation, a kind of compromise procedure has become accepted as not essentially different from direct carving, and thus a very widely accepted way of creating sculptures in stone. By this procedure the sculptor makes, first, a clay model, from this, a plaster cast and finally copies his own plaster cast into

32

stone. As a method, aiming to produce a vital work of art, this is scarcely better than the worst nineteenth-century practice.

While there are many fundamental objections to this practice of a subtle nature, two obvious ones stand out. The first is the one that it shares with, what I have called, the nineteenth-century procedure. It is, that forms produced by manipulating clay have, at every point, a special character imparted to them by the kind of movements of the hands, one might say the gestures, that go with building up in a soft material. This stems inevitably from the condition that the human mind does not float in a vacuum, willing things into existence; it has to operate through a body. Conversely, the quality of the forms that arise from the diametrically opposed activity of carving stone have likewise, at every point, their own special character. Whatever the general similarity of the ideas which may have existed in the mind, this is inescapable. The absurdity of trying first to work out in clay the forms for stone is obvious. The secondhandedness involved and the redundancy of the procedure is also obvious. The second of the objections is the difficulty of maintaining the fire of enthusiasm and inspiration through a process of working out the whole thing twice, once in clay, then in stone. Gifted artists may occasionally have overcome the disadvantages of the indirect method of making sculpture in stone to produce some worthy works; but why submit oneself to the obstructiveness of a method so fundamentally frustrating to the process of communication through art?

The process of direct carving, as I see it, consists first in choosing a block of stone having the kind of qualities calculated to respond to the sculptor's mood and ideas at the time. Then, with no thought of intermediate operations in any other kind of material, to take tools to it and carve it. Thus to work it until it comes as near as possible to expressing those ideas prevailing in the sculptor's mind. If the sculptor works on the stone in the right frame of mind it will express more than can be evoked by the mere general form and disposition of the planes and masses. I mean by this, such as the shapes alone could express on a sort of 'least common denominator' level however they might be generated and in whatever material. Worked with the right attitude of mind the sculpture can and will display, in addition to the expressiveness of the design, what I have earlier called a kind of fossilization in stone of characteristic movement and gesture. So it gets the power to evoke the special responses belonging to its particular sphere. This is an aspect of the proper exploitation of stone as a material.* Another of the advantages pertaining to direct

33

carving is that the artist himself controls everything from the veriest raw material to the finished article. He starts from a block of stone no more than dragged out of the earth by other men. From this, purely by the labours of his own hands, he makes the finished thing. Here no 'middlemen', no dependence on others, and no intermediate processes blur the immediacy of communication. In the Book of Genesis it says: 'in the sweat of thy face shalt thou eat bread', and it is likewise that sculpture must be made. To be of the best and really significant, sculpture must be anointed with sweat.

I do not want to leave the introductory part of the book without pointing out advantages which, from the practical point of view, stone sculpture has over metal sculpture for the embellishment of buildings. Obviously the appearance of stone sculpture tends to harmonize better with buildings themselves constructed of stone or clad in stone. It also frequently does so where buildings are constructed of concrete or even of brick. Quite apart from questions of aesthetics, technical matters contribute. Sculpture in steel or iron quickly disfigures buildings with festoons of staining by rust. Those of bronze often cause a similar kind of corrosion stains on stone which spread over the face of the building.

Regarding the range of work for which stone is most suitable, it includes, at one end of the scale, large and up to colossal figures on buildings and memorials. In the intermediate range come smaller figures and portrait busts and heads, placed indoors. The smaller end of the scale is represented by such things as portable stone carvings like the ritual mask shown in figure 65.

Finally, developing the theme of some observations I made earlier about many of the sculpture departments of schools of art, the potential direct carver is at little disadvantage if his circumstances prevent him from attending one. For instance, Eric Gill, famous sculptor as he was, had at no time been to an art school sculpture department. Also, later, he developed an extremely successful school of direct carving of his own having scarcely any resemblance to a conventional school of art. I would say that there are advantages and disadvantages either way and so no reader need despair because geographical or other circumstances prevent him getting to a regular school of art. In my opinion one who wants to be a direct carver in stone misses nothing of value to him if he misses that all-too-dominant modelling from life class of the art school curriculum. One of the main things a student needs is plenty of drawing from life of the right kind which most individuals or small groups can organize anywhere for

34

themselves. If he can get this in a regular art school so much the easier. The chances are that he will receive good teaching in drawing from life in a school of art. Those who want the right education in direct carving should eliminate from their curriculum modelling from life and all other modelling. From the very start they should do no work in three dimensions except stone carving. The education in stone carving should follow a course similar to that which I shall set out in the following pages with reasonable variations to allow for the individuality of student or of teacher.

On the foundation indicated a structure of education can be built which, as I later point out, can have few failures because each student goes as far on the path as his inborn capacities permit. But at all levels the work has value and applications. It escapes the grim and unwholesome prospect which tends to dominate the painting school, the alternatives of reaching either recognition of creative genius or despair. It also has advantages for the student who can only be a part-timer or who is unlikely to make sculpting his main profession.

The student must exercise himself in two separate but closely co-ordinated activities; drawing from life and practising stone carving.

CHAPTER TWO

MINIMUM TOOL AND MATERIAL NEEDS

BANKERS OR CARVING STANDS

This is the support on which the stone carving is worked. It needs to be strong and heavy to give solid support against the weight of the stone and the violence of the work. It must be the right height to suit the sculptor's own height. The work is done in a lower relative position than modelling and most mechanical jobs. It must not be much more bulky than the block of stone and must be placed so that the sculptor can work equally well all round it. A basic height of about 2 feet to 2 feet 6 inches is usually convenient. An ordinary work bench or a modelling stand are for different reasons not convenient. A very suitable and often easy-to-get thing is the stump end, or drum, cut out of a tree trunk—oak, elm or ash preferably. It should be sawn flat top and bottom, and to the height recommended. A student can manage very well to begin with on a small but strong 'used' packing crate about 2 feet 6 inches × 2 feet × 2 feet. Pack it up inside with pieces of stone or other weighty things to make it steady. Sculptors usually follow the custom of masons by making the minor adjustments to working height by means of paired up pieces of hardwood, added to the basic height of the main banker; these are also called bankers. They are usually carpenter's discards, odd end pieces of baulks of timber. As opportunity occurs sculptors and masons collect them and all the wooden wedges they can. My illustration on figure 49 shows the most convenient kind of stand for small work, in a group of studio kit to be acquired as it becomes needed.

LIGHT

The sculptor must have a top light, or near top light and the more general and diffused, or non-directional, it is the better. Daylight out-of-doors is the ideal.

TOOLS IN GENERAL

Sculpture tools are basically the same as those used in the stone-mason's craft, with some slight refinements here and there. They are

37

10. Working in a typical granite mason's yard in Cornwall. The author after his college of art training learned the basic technique of stone carving in a yard like this one. Note: on the left, a block of granite, which has been split, being taken a stage further with the heavy point; on the right, two men working with the set and driving hammer. (*See* Chapter X. Granite Carving and Stone Splitting)

to be bought from sculptors' and masons' tool-sellers. These can be found in most chief cities and very commonly in neighbourhoods where stonework is a local industry. Their names and addresses are also likely to be found in art magazines or can be discovered by enquiries at art materials shops, etc.

The following is the minimum required by a beginner, and further on in the book I shall add a supplementary list.

HAMMERS

The best kind of hammers for limestone, sandstone and marble are the special sculpture hammers. These are lump hammers with heads made of annealed iron, not of steel. Nevertheless, it is possible to make do quite well with ordinary ironmongers' steel lump hammers. In fact, for heavy roughing out I myself use these or granite hammers,

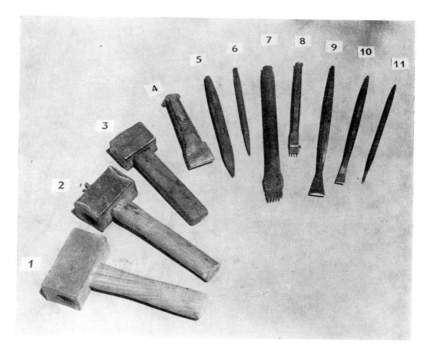

11. Marble tools: 1, 2 and 3, iron hammers; 4, pitcher; 5, heavy point; 6, light point; 7 and 8, claw-bits in holders; 9, 10 and 11, chisels—broad to narrow

which are also of steel, for reasons of economy. To begin with, a relatively heavy and a light one are needed. The student must find out what weight of head suits his strength. As his arms become strengthened by the work he will step up the weight he liked to use, with a resulting improvement in his stone-cutting rate. To begin with, about 2 pounds for the heavier and 1 pound for the lighter one. As the student becomes experienced he is likely to step up to about 4 pounds for heavy roughing out. There is no point in having a special iron hammer at this weight.

POINTS

These are the tools with which most of the work is done. They are a sort of punch with a cutting end forged and ground to a sharp pyramid shape. The butt end is a sort of truncated cone. There are two kinds of cutting ends, a purely pyramidal point (which I personally always use) and a kind of flattened point, a little chisel-like, for use with softer stones. The first is called a marble point and the

39

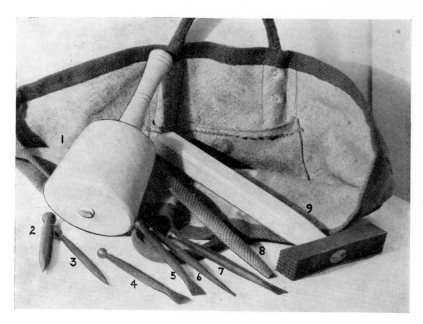

12. Stone tools: 1, mallet; 2 and 3 heavy and light points; 4, claw tool; 5, 6 and 7, chisels, broad to narrow; 8, stone rasp; 9, Bouchard hammer. Note the shape of the butt ends of tools 2-7 an obvious difference from the marble hammer head tools

second a stone point. There are also two types of butt ends. The one I have already described is called a marble tool, or cup-headed, and the other, which has a big flattened butt, is called a stone tool or alternatively mallet-headed. The latter is, of course, for use only with a mallet, if you prefer one to a hammer. Wooden mallets are for use with softer limestones but I personally have no use for them.

Points start about 8 inches long and get shorter as they are re-sharpened until they become unusable. Points are made in two sizes, heavy and light. The heavy are usually forged from $\frac{5}{8}$ inch diameter octagonal steel bar, and the light ones from $\frac{7}{16}$ inch. I would like to point out here to the student that the shape, size and weight of tools is the product of hundreds of years' experience of their use. He needs three or four of each size to begin with. He would need only one of each size but that he must have a few spare ones for use while others are being sharpened.

CHISELS

Sculptors' chisels are somewhat like what engineers and ironmongers call 'cold chisels'. The difference is that for limestone, sandstone and marble they are forged up to a more refined shape. For granite the shape is almost the same as a cold chisel, but they must be of a superior steel and a different 'temper' from ordinary cold chisels. All that I have said about the butt ends of points applies similarly to chisels and I shall not repeat it, but refer the reader back. Chisels are usually forged relatively a little longer than points. A beginner will need about two of each width of cutting edge, from about $\frac{3}{16}$ inch, up to about 1 inch.

CLAW TOOL OR CLAW BIT AND HOLDER

The original form of this tool was the claw tool, but the claw bit and holder is one of the few new inventions among sculptors' tools. A claw tool is like a chisel with a cutting edge serrated like saw teeth. In fact, it is forged up in just the same way as a chisel, the dents are then cut and after this they are hardened and tempered. The claw bit and holder is an economical substitute for a claw tool. It consists of two separate parts: the holder, shaped like the bulk of a chisel with a wedge-shaped slot socket at the working end; plus the claw bit, made to fit into the socket of the holder. The claw bit has a double row of dents arranged back to back. It is used until worn out one way and then turned round in the holder. It is not quite so pleasant to use as a claw tool but much more economical. A beginner, in my opinion, only needs the finer dents, bit width $\frac{1}{2}$ inch: one holder and, say, a dozen bits.

PITCHERS

These are the tools with which the bolder roughing out is done. They are like an extremely robust, wide edged and stumpy chisel. They have no cutting edge as has a chisel, but a bevelled edge. The width of the working edge is about $1\frac{1}{2}$ inches and whereas a chisel has a sharp edge these have a thick-edge of about $\frac{1}{4}$ inch in the form of a bevel. As they are slow to wear out only one of these tools is needed.

SHARPENING EQUIPMENT

Points, chisels and claw tools need frequent sharpening. The amount of sharpening required is in accordance with the kind of stone used. With granite or hard grit stones a great deal, a tediously great deal, of sharpening is needed. With limestones and marbles far less is required. The sharpening is done by grinding the cutting edge or

41

13. Tool sharpening by grinding. Remember to cool the tool frequently by dipping in water during the operation. Note the horizontal grinding wheel

point. After much grinding away of the tool in sharpening it becomes too obtuse for further use. It then has to be re-forged, hardened and tempered by a skilled toolsmith. This is called fire-sharpening. It makes the tool like new again except for being a little shorter and needing the initial grinding for working sharpness.

The grinding used to be done on the old-fashioned type of natural grit stone grindstone in which the large wheel passed, during each revolution, through water in a trough at the bottom. This had the great advantage that the wheel and thus also the tool, was kept cool by the water. Most people now use a high revving carborundum wheel driven by a treadle or electrical power or, in the cheapest kind, by a handle and gearing. The carborundum grinding wheel is usually about 5 inches in diameter. There is a particularly well-designed treadle-driven carborundum grinding wheel sold in Britain. It is specially made for masons, and well worth the moderate extra cost against a handle grinder. Electrical power-driven grinders have no advantage over it. The student has to have one of these alternative ways of grinding tools unless he proposes to limit himself to working in the softer grades of limestone when he might make do with a carborundum rubbing stone.

For the fire-sharpening mentioned earlier the student has the alternatives of sending them back to his supplier, or finding a conveniently located toolsmith who can do the job, or if he lives in some place remote from such conveniences, learn to do it himself. I shall assume that he can get the tools fire-sharpened in the usual way and confine myself to some instructions about grinding which will come later in the book.

This kit is not composed of things special to sculpture. A ruler is needed and the most convenient kind is a mason's rust-proofed steel rule 2 to 3 feet long. A steel set-square must be got and the type made for masons which is also rust-proofed is the best, size about $1\frac{1}{2}$ feet $\times$ 1 foot. The student will have to get a pair of metal callipers with legs about 1 foot long. Add an ordinary set of mechanical drawing instruments, a strong pair of scissors and drawing pencils.

CHAPTER THREE

THE RIGHT ATTITUDE OF MIND
IN WHICH TO BEGIN STONE CARVING

I most strongly believe that the rationale of successful training in direct carving in stone is the right approach. There are no gimmicks to be easily and quickly picked up in this sphere. In general, as an attitude to learning, I most strongly disapprove of it; and sculpture is a field in which it is particularly inappropriate. On the other hand, by the methods advocated herein the climb through to the stage of producing figure subjects and works of art in general is interesting and rewarding all the way. It is a process of education which can have no failures among those with a genuine feeling for stone. Those without, will discover the fact at an early stage and drop out in a natural way. All this grows out of the proper exploitation of some special advantages happily possessed by the craft of stone carving. There is a most beneficial relationship and an uninterrupted progression between the masons' craft of stone carving and sculpture in its subtle fine art form.

Seemingly it is not possible for, say, painters to enjoy the benefits of any parallel sodality between the men who paint woodwork on buildings and the men who paint works of art.

The late Eric Gill and his School carried the exploitation of this happy circumstance to the excessive degree of making of it a positive fetish. Many people found this increasingly unacceptable and a hostile reaction was consequently produced, which I hope to correct. I advocate taking advantage of this most helpful and wholesome factor enjoyed exclusively by the art of sculpture in stone, without allowing it the excessively dominant role assigned to it by the Gill School.

CHAPTER FOUR

HOW THE SCULPTOR IN STONE
MAY BEST USE THE LIFE MODEL

The student must exercise himself in two separate but co-ordinated activities; drawing from life and stone carving.

The methods of drawing from life set out here form one part of the process of education which will liberate the student from the tyranny of prototype copying into stone which continues to be the general practice for work embodying a predominently representational element.

The sculpture student who, as I recommend, is making drawing his recourse to the life model, must develop a rather special way of drawing. If he attends the life drawing class in a school of art he must get all he can out of the instruction given. However, he will be unlikely to find that it is attuned to his special needs. It will, most likely, be given by a teacher whose outlook is that of a painter and so the student will have to modify his drawing to suit his own particular requirements, at the same time profiting as much as possible from the instruction he is receiving.

This kind of drawing from life that the sculpture student needs to make should be representative of actual three-dimensional form and tending away from the aesthetic principles of expressionism, that is, the student should exert all his powers to make his drawings a clear statement of the form in three dimensions and should completely ignore the tonal aspect arising from the colour of the model and also the ideas involved in expressionism. He should not concern himself with linear rhythms or the direct expressiveness of line appreciated from a calligraphic point of view. Line in-its-own-right should not be emphasized but only in the way that it can contribute to the elucidation of the three-dimensional form.

Something that has been completely neglected in modern times may, most profitably, be revived in this connection. I refer to the theoretical and experimental work on the subject of chiaroscuro by Leonardo da Vinci in the fifteenth century. The student would get much benefit from the study of Leonardo's notes on this subject. I will, herein, go as far as I may in providing a brief introduction to

45

the revival of the exploitation of the principles of chiaroscuro. I suggest that a further study of it be pursued when possible. I feel I should here point out that anyone at the present time embarking on these studies will find himself in the company of a very small band of pioneers and is unlikely to experience much sympathy or understanding from the majority of his contemporaries. As the sculpture student is, at least at this stage, not concerned with exhibiting drawings, this is of little consequence. This state of affairs arises from the present predominance of a certain ruling vogue in the field of drawing. This is to be concerned almost exclusively with linear rhythms and the aforementioned calligraphic qualities of line. Where tone is employed it is in a manner analogous to that of the decorative spots used in calligraphy, as foil to the cursive strokes. This is the attitude which governs the character of most contemporary drawing and one not adapted to our special needs.

In his drawing the beginner sculptor will find that he derives much advantage from adopting a theoretical system of chiaroscuro and adhering to it in most cases; one designed to explain the form and being very little influenced by the, possibly, rather random accidental pattern of light and shade presented by the appearance of the model. He should find the exploitation of such a system of light and shade more fruitful than experiments with contour.

A good system of chiaroscuro to choose is one built on the assumption that the light revealing the form of the model is falling on the model in a downwards direction at an angle of about 45° and also inclined obliquely to the direction of vision at about the same angle. This may either be from half-right or from half-left according to individual preference. This particular set-up determines that those planes on the model which face upwards at an angle of 45° and simultaneously are oblique to the direction of vision at an angle of 45° are the ones that receive the maximum of illumination. Planes at all other angles receive less illumination according to a scale of gradation which it is not difficult to work out. Such a system makes it possible to fix precisely the position in space of a plane by the gradation of tone used to represent it according to this exact code. To this must, of course, be added its relative position on the drawing paper and the containing effect of contour. In this way is produced a clear record of any passage of form either seen on the model or, in the case of a memory drawing, imaged.

After some practice with a simplified system of chiaroscuro such as the foregoing the student may introduce, first cast shadow and then

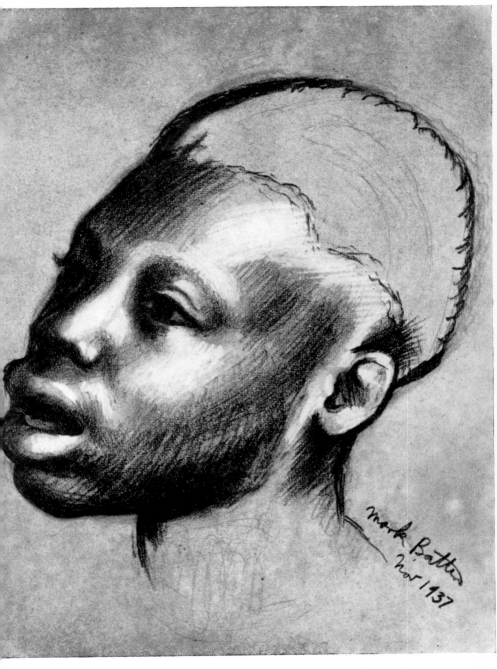

14. Quick sketch study from life—one of the series done for the sculpture *Singing Negress*, shown at various stages of the carving in figures 43 to 46. In chalk on toned paper it is of the kind described in the text as a stage in the method of approaching sculpture by the direct carving technique without modelling preparation

15. Study from life, Mary B.-B.2. Life-size tone drawing of the kind described in the text as one of the preliminary stages suitable for approaching the carving of stone sculpture without any modelling preparation

16. These two interconnected diagrams, of a kind described in the text, are representative examples from a series of diagrammatic studies for the sculpture *Sir Edmund Craster*, on the Bodleian Library at Oxford. This sculpture is shown at different stages of the work in figures 40 to 42. Experimentally taking this kind of section from the life model in the mechanical manner described in the text, in conjunction with the kind of drawing from life described, should form part of the direct carver's education. An education devised to free him from dependence on modelling as a preparation for carving. Later on it will not be necessary nor, furthermore would it be practicably convenient to take such sections mechanically from a sitter for a portrait. When trained, the sculptor will be able to draw this type of section spontaneously and creatively from observation only from the model. In the diagrams note: the indications of the outlines of the block of stone, the hoodmoulding and the face of the wall; the way in which the forward and downward inclination of the head is fixed; the way in which the sideways rotation of the head in relation to the wall surface is fixed; that the neck incorporates a turn shown by numbers 5 and 6 of the sections and axial lines. The numbered lines on the profile, or vertical, section indicate the positions at which the sections shown on the other diagram are taken and are their traces. These positions are chosen as the ones which most determine the characteristics of the head

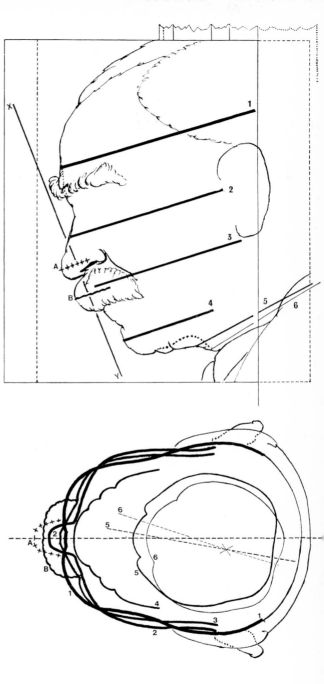

49

reflected light. This will increase the interest of the drawings and if carefully used supplement their expressiveness as records of the form.

In cases where the student can contrive the actual lighting of the life studio and position of the model and his direction of vision to accord with his adopted system of chiaroscuro he will find this helpful. However, it is neither necessary not even desirable always to arrange this. In cases where he cannot do this he must ignore the rather random pattern of light and shade which the appearance of the model usually presents and impose his adopted system. Although this is a very difficult exercise it is at the same time a very stimulating one to reject completely the pattern of light and dark presented by the model and arbitrarily employ a quite different scheme to record the shape of the forms and their relationships. Obviously, later on, other systems of chiaroscuro should be experimented with. It should be noted that the example given above has certain advantages, one of which is that the drawings will exhibit the beneficial characteristic of having a wide band of dark tone mainly on one side counterbalanced by a narrower band of lighter tone on the other. Practically all the contours will be supported by a fringing band of tone on the inside of them.

If the sculpture student lapses into making drawings which are merely thoughtless, semi-photographic, reproductions of the chequer of tones and lines presented by the appearance of the model he will be neither exercising his mind in the right way nor building up the library of records of form which are the reasons for his being in the life studio. Very soon, all the drawings that do not entirely fail should be saved and kept in some sort of reference order, as the supplement to the stone carving branch of activity which they are destined to be.

Another special characteristic of the kind of life drawings that should be made by the beginner at sculpture is one concerned with silhouette. I will try to make this clearer by expressing it as relating to the horizons presented by the surfaces as they turn out of view. Most people grow rigidly accustomed, to a degree unsuspected, to the silhouettes displayed to the eye of a standing or sitting spectator by figures themselves in the upright or the sitting position. They realize this acutely when the model is posed in some very unfamiliar relationship to the eye, and they do not experience any of the customary reactions of the pattern represented. These silhouettes under consideration are in fact the edges of two-dimensional sections taken through the three-dimensional form and the point to note is that they are all developed within approximately vertical planes. This is the mind's

customary diet of visual phenomena which is very closely and indis-
solubly linked to a great part of our emotional reactions.

In order to develop in himself a much more thorough understanding
of the shape of the form in three dimensions I recommend the student
to embark on an intensive study of the sections of the figure taken in
horizontal planes. I should say, not planes necessarily horizontal, but
planes perpendicular to the main or central axis of that part of the
form under examination. To elucidate, imagine lines drawn round
parts of the figure in a plane perpendicular to the axial line as they
would be seen by an eye looking in a direction concurrent with the
axial line. The sections thus developed are the more significant ones
for the sculptor. The study of them is more profitable to him than
that of the silhouettes of vertical planes with which we are all very
familiar. When drawing it is necessary continually to sustain the
action of carrying these two types of sections simultaneously in the
mind. This is part of the way in which to escape from the copying
of the familiar silhouette in a state of mind dominated by the reactions
which much conditioning has brought us.

One effective practical aid to the study of these sections perpendicular to the main axes is that based on the use of pieces of lead
or lead alloy wire of about $\frac{1}{8}$ or $\frac{3}{16}$ inch in thickness. This wire is
easy to bend, has no springiness, and can be straightened again with
the same facility. This makes it possible to take pieces of suitable
lengths and to press them on to the form of the model. Where
necessary they can be first bent, offered up, and bent again, until they
exactly fit the form. By this trial and error process they can be made
exactly to reproduce the shape of the model. A large sheet of cartoon
paper should have been prepared in order to receive the sections,
drawing-pinned conveniently to the floor or to a large drawing board
placed near the model. By careful manipulation the bent wire can
be transferred to the paper and a trace made from it in pencil. In
working, care should be taken to check the dimension across the
mouth of the U-shaped section of wire before making the trace.
This should be done by taking the dimension off the model with
callipers. By using with ingenuity a plumb line and drawing instruments the sections can be plotted on the paper in their relative
positions. Generally speaking, a vertical distance of about 8 inches
between the sections taken is suitable. It is usually better to vary this
a little to take in the more significant parts then to operate at measured
regular intervals. A kind of analysis of the form is produced by this
process which always proves extremely illuminating.

One further point is that a student will find it advantageous to practice this work on the plaster casts from the antique (often part of the equipment of schools of art). He will find his results teach him much even here and he will gain, at the same time, practice in making the process work accurately, smoothly, and without errors.

CHAPTER FIVE

CHOOSING THE MOST SUITABLE THINGS WITH WHICH TO BEGIN STONE CARVING

The foregoing section, on drawing from life, describes the less special part of the regimen which will free the student from the tyranny of copying prototypes into stone where work of a representational nature is the aim. This, the main part of the regimen, involves the decisive and drastic method of abandoning modelling once and for all, as soon as a student has decided to become a carver of sculpture in stone. Ideally, he should never again form a shape in clay. He must now start to mount step by step, gaining experience and confidence in the process of carving shapes in stone; shapes selected so that their accuracy is verifiable by measurement and which are reasonably within his powers at each stage of his work. He must firmly put from him the absurdity, apparently so tempting, of trying to achieve the complexities involved in creating a work of art, before he has learned the basic mason's ability to produce in stone with sureness the shapes intended.

The student has no cause to regard this prospect with dismay because if he is a person likely to become a good sculptor he will obviously take far less time than an apprentice mason to acquire all that he needs of a mason's proficiency. It is right for him to move on to each further stage because he has yet acquired anything like a mason's speed and before he has quite reached a mason's high standard of purely geometrical accuracy. In other words, he need not be held back to the conservative tempo of the training routine of an apprentice mason. On the other hand, in his natural eagerness to get on he must not allow himself to disregard reasonable standards of mechanical accuracy. The necessary speed he can gain while working at the more advanced stages.

We now come to the point of selecting the kind of object suitable for a first carving and of designing it. At this stage the student should put right out of his mind the kind of thing which is usually

53

17. Trough in Sussex sandstone. The very first exercise in stone carving by the author in his youth. Notice his choice of geometrical and conventional shapes, with no attempt at work of art, although he had been exhibiting drawings and paintings for several years

considered as in the category of a work of fine art. Turn instead for inspiration and guidance to that abundance of delightful things carved in stone which are usually considered to be works of applied art. Call to mind all the architectural ornament that is to be seen on Egyptian, Classical, Romanesque, Gothic and Renaissance buildings. Dwell on the capitals, keystones, brackets, gargoyles, sarcophagi, tombs, fonts, bosses, pendants, finials, well-heads, etc. These things were, generally speaking, the work of masons only just below the level of sculptors. As I have already pointed out, there is here to be found fortunately no definite dividing line like there is between the men who paint doors and the men who paint works of art. While the student should follow his fancy in this matter there are good reason to turn, for one, to that Golden Age of masonry and sculpture, the Romanesque Period in Northern Europe, including Britain. A student who has already become interested in stone and stone carving has only to enter a cathedral or almost any old church in Britain or another part of Northern Europe to become absorbed, delighted and, it must be, inspired to stone carving activity.

54

18. *Coptic niche*, seventh century. The actual stone carving involved in creating this exquisite thing would be within the powers of a beginner or an amateur (British Museum, Crown copyright)

It is an advantage of our times that those who have not physical access to the kind of things they need to study have the useful substitute of photographs and museum examples.

Those students whose interest in art has already led them to art galleries where their taste has made them feel most drawn to the semi-representational or to the completely abstract types of work should, even so, not be prejudiced against the course of education here proposed. The reason being that ideas drawn from first impressions produced by such work are liable to be very mistaken. Those who want to do work of that kind should realize that a thorough education in the craft of stone carving is in fact as essential for that field as for any other. So also is the acquisition of an abundant vocabulary of form which can only be acquired from the study of natural appearances supplemented by study of the products of other people's digestion of them. It is a good form for the student's educa-

55

tion to take to make his development something of a microcosm of the evolution of art.

All this having been considered, let the student take a moderate-sized piece of limestone of one of the softer kinds. Here I must digress to point out that the necessary information about the chemistry, physics and geographical distribution of stones suitable for sculpture appears in a later chapter. I suggest a piece of stone having a volume of, very roughly, one cubic foot; of course, I do not mean necessarily a cube of one foot: it may be any shape. It is worth noting here that a piece of stone of this size will weigh somewhere between 130 and 180 pounds.

Next decide what to carve from it. In thinking out this design for a first stone carving, try to combine in it something which will be interesting to make, attractive to keep and afford the necessary kind of practice in carving. The first thing to be tried should have some flat surfaces, rectangular planes, rectangular intersections, some curved surfaces, some repetition, and so on. Figure 17 is a reproduction of the first piece of stone I myself took tools to. It was a small shallow trough which could be used for growing rock plants or cacti in, or otherwise as a garden ornament. It was not an attempt at a work of art. As you may see, it was a conventional Gothic type of design but gave plenty of scope for practice at stone carving and at accurate setting out. The shapes to be carved were geometrical, varied, with also some repetition; but most important of all they could be measured and proved right or wrong; it had no vague shapes that could not be checked. The student should invent for himself something having these necessary properties and which can be contained by the dimensions of the piece of stone he has obtained.

I will follow with some suggestions for things that a student could well make while he is acquiring the necessary ability at stone carving. Without going into improper competition with any local tradesmen masons, the beginner might make for himself, or to give away, a goodly variety of objects at the applied art level while he is learning to be able to carve stone well enough eventually to create sculpture. Although this idea may appear shockingly unlike anything customarily contemplated by art students I hold the view that it is much more wholesome and far less frustrating for everybody concerned than the usual practice of the art schools. I refer to the, at present, almost universal practice in the schools, of learning even the most elementary part of stone carving while making things supposedly to be looked upon as attempts at works of art. While this can be attempted, to

19. English Romanesque capital. Peterborough Cathedral. Notice the ingenuity of this fine design, with what simple means the effect has been created. The stone carving skill demanded does not go beyond a fairly elementary stage and the ingenuity of the design should stimulate student or amateur to invent similar things

some extent, at the more advanced stages it is absurdly impractical to try to do it at the elementary stages. It has the further disadvantage that the kind of objects being carved do not usually embody shapes that can be tested by measurement. Thus they do not fulfil the basic essential of first practice pieces. I suggest, therefore, the selection of things like the following for first attempts: stone doorstops; a great variety of garden ornaments, such as simple urns for plants; traditional 'poppyhead' or 'pineapple' finials to put on terraces; stone troughs, based on the designs of fonts or sarcophagi or well-heads, for growing plants in. There is no end to the simple and attractive things of this sort that can be devised which will give some pleasure even when not perfect in workmanship. For a later stage capitals, brackets, or keystones, could be carved and inserted into buildings, or built-in, in cases where cost would not have allowed a tradesman's work to be incorporated in the building. For the later stages, before being able to embark upon figure sculpture, such things as stone fireplaces, or tomb-stones could be made. These are only a few suggestions to set the student's own mind working. For inspiration in design he will find Roman and Renaissance architectural ornament a very fruitful source, but, above all, the exciting detail to be found in cathedrals and churches of the Romanesque period. Material of this sort provides much better training in direct carving in stone than do immature attempts to make works of art of nebulous shape. There is in it a quite sufficient degree of interest to keep up enthusiasm, while the main emphasis can be on the practical side, the carving of definite shapes which can be checked by measurement for correctness.

This provides that both student and master can judge progress and future needs.

20. English Romanesque capital in the crypt of Canterbury Cathedral. As carving, easily within the ability of a student or an amateur at an early stage

21. English Romanesque capital. Twyford (Berks.)

22. English Romanesque capital. St. Peter's (Northants.)

23. English Romanesque font. Hodnet. Very simple to carve, fine proportion and feeling for stone in the design

24. Italian well-head in marble, tenth century. A beautiful design but needing only carving skill at a fairly elementary stage (Victoria and Albert Museum, Crown copyright.)

25. Romanesque fragment. Winchester Cathedral. As stone carving a work like this leads to a further stage

26. French Romanesque capital. Chartres Cathedral. An outstandingly fine work from the points of view both of design and of stone carving. All these Romanesque works demonstrate the benefit arising from the fact that the designer and the carver are the same person (*see* pages 6 and 7)

27. English Romanesque font. Castle Froome, Hereford

28. English Romanesque font. Shernborne (Norfolk)

29. English Medieval font. Bodmin (Cornwall)

30. Ancient Central American coiled snake in polished stone (Courtesy British Museum, Crown copyright)

31. Ancient Egyptian design of ram in granite (Courtesy British Museum, Crown copyright)

32. Italian Romanesque, base of a column of the eleventh century. These last few examples mark the stage for the student of advancing to work fully in the round and free-standing. They are shown here to stimulate the student to invent ideas of his own at this level

CHAPTER SIX

HOW TO USE THE BASIC KIT OF STONE CARVING TOOLS

I belong to that school of sculptors which believes that as much work as possible should be done with the point, heavy and light. I consider it to be the sculptor's main tool.

Take up a heavy point in the left hand and a hammer of about 2 pounds weight in the right. The point should be held firmly on the surface of the stone in a suitable place and the blow struck. The general principle is that the point is driven in under the stone and cracks a piece off. The angle to the stone at which the tool is held is decisive and the correct one only learned by experience, but some general guidance can give a useful start. The best angle varies for the different kinds of stone. It varies from about 40° to about 60° to the face of the stone. The more acute angle 40° to 50° is that used for limestones and softer grades of sandstones (or grit-stones as they are sometimes called). The steeper (or more obtuse) angle, round about 60°, is that used for very hard stones such as granite. The reason that the tool is held at a more steep angle on granite is that otherwise it would not 'grip'; it would merely skid on the surface of the very hard stone, doing no work. The beginner must experiment by varying the angle to the stone at which he holds the tool until he finds the most efficient one for the particular material he is working on (I have earlier suggested a softer limestone for his first work). If the tool skids or does not 'bite' deeply enough he is holding it at too acute an angle to the surface. On the other hand, he will know when he is holding it too steeply (or obtusely) for the kind of stone in work because it will 'draw' into the stone. This means that the tool will drive into the stone and stick fast like a nail in wood instead of cracking off flakes of stone as it should do. Alternatively it will just make holes in the stone without splitting any off. This result could otherwise be the outcome of another fault in working which I will refer to farther on. The former fault

33. Demonstrating the heavy point

cannot be long continued without resulting in the whole sharp end
of the tool breaking off at a point about an ½ inch back from the tip.

Although sculpture tools may appear very simple and even
crude, in fact their size and relative proportions are the outcome
of ages of experiment and experience. Thus while a great deal of
what I state may seem very arbitrary and positive there is no point
in anyone experimenting for himself in fields where experiment
by forerunners has long ago settled on the best arrangement.

Regarding the hammer blow, more than one blow is commonly
applied without repositioning the tip of the tool. This is a matter of
individual habit; but the rhythm—tap, tap, pause, tap, tap, pause—
is one quite commonly to be heard coming from mason's yard or
sculptor's studio. Masons and sculptors use a hammer heavier in the
head than carpenters or engineers but proportionately shorter in
the handle; they also customarily grip it much nearer the head than
do the latter, who usually grip the handle right at its end. One of the

first things that the beginner will discover is that he quite often mis-hits and hits his hand instead of the butt of the tool. When he does so he usually hits the first knuckle of his thumb. Most students soon get over this stage but it must be admitted that it can cause a painful state of the hand while it goes on. During the period of working through this stage the student may find that he has to wear a thick leather (such as horse-hide) glove on his left hand; or perhaps manage with a thick leather thumb-stall. He should get rid of it as soon as he can afford to do so. In masons' yards much chaffing of the apprentices goes on about this.

The experienced sculptor develops to the state of not being consciously aware of having hands or of hitting the tool with the hammer. He must be able to concentrate his attention exclusively on the tip of the tool and the surface of the stone and the behaviour of the stone at the point of impact. It is a necessary preliminary mastery that has to be acquired; also the ability continually to vary the angle of the tool while all the time true-hitting the butt with the hammer quite automatically, without having to give any part of the attention to it. This proficiency must be acquired in order to be able to adjust the angle of the tool to the different angles called for by the roughness of the surface of the stone.

It must be borne in mind that for even the very best hardened tempered steel, to 'cut' stone is something of the utmost limit of its capacity. This is particularly so when granite or very hard grit-stone is the material. The mineral substance of which grit-stone is composed and the majority of those composing granite are, in fact, considerably harder than the steel itself. The reader will the more fully realize this when I point out that the old-fashioned type of large grind-stone which was until modern times the only thing available to be used for grinding steel, for such purposes as tool sharpening, was itself made of natural grit-stone. This kind of hard grit-stone is occasionally used as a material for sculpture to which it gives the utmost possible degree of durability at the cost of arduous labour. *Mermaid* and *Allegorical Head* were carved in this kind of stone, see figures 4 and 80. In the case of these very hard stones it is only by exploiting steel's superior toughness against the stone's superior hardness that carving can be achieved at all. The same applies if to a much less degree, to the carving of softer stones. In the case of the harder stones, without skill one may only too easily batter the tools to destruction with little effect on the stone. The foregoing is all leading to the point of showing that the sculptor must

74

search the stone before him and plan his assault on it in the best way to get results. Only experience can teach him the kinds of ways in which stone yields but correct early guidance in this, as in any other field, greatly speeds up the process of learning.

In general, projections, angles, edges etc, yield the most easily. When carving this principle must be exploited to the maximum. It follows, therefore, that the middle parts of flat surfaces or the hollows are the places where the most resistance will be encountered. The student increases his difficulties unnecessarily if he gets the surface in too smooth a condition while he has still a lot of stone to get off. One principle of working with the point is, do not drive at an 'up hill' slope because the stone you are trying to remove is all the time buttressed by other stone and will not yield. This is the other fault referred to earlier which causes the tool to 'draw' into the stone. Work the other way round; cut at a 'falling away' slope and work it back. While in reading this may seem a little obscure, as soon as the student puts tool to stone he will understand what is meant.

Never just bang away at the stone in a random unplanned way. At each stage consider carefully what has next to be done and think out the best way to achieve it and work methodically. For instance, when taking the work down with the heavy point, which is what we are now considering, first decide how much stone needs to be taken off using the particular tool in hand. Second, decide how many drafts or stints carried right over the surface will be needed to remove this much. Then work right over the whole surface of that part of the work taking off everywhere one layer. The thickness of this layer is determined by the average amount of stone that comes off at one tooling. Work right over the surface each time taking off an even layer of stone until enough has been carved away to have taken the work down to the stage of requiring the next kind of tool. Do not wander about on stone hunting the likely looking projections to split off; and taking the more off where it comes more easily.

WORKING WITH THE PITCHER

It may strike the reader as a little strange that I should have described working with the point before I described working with the pitcher when, in fact, the use of the pitcher comes first in reducing the stone. I have done this because it is better for the beginner to start his experiments with the point than with the pitcher.

The pitcher is the tool with which one does the heavy roughing out on limestones, the softer grades of grit-stones and marble. Its shape

34. Demonstrating the pitcher on the edge of a block

has already been described on page 41. The pitcher, which is used in conjunction with the heavier hammer, operates most efficiently when taking off stone working from the angles and corners of the block. By this I mean where two approximately flat surfaces intersect at more or less than a right angle such as commonly occurs at the natural edges and corners of a block of stone. At such positions, working with average limestone, it is usual with the pitcher to split off roughly wedge-shaped pieces of stone of about the bulk of a man's hand. In order to get this effect the student should start from a corner of the stone, and place the pitcher in position leaving about 1 inch between the adjacent end of the working edge of the pitcher and the corner of the stone. The pitcher should be held at right angles to that face of the stone with which it is in contact and its working edge should be parallel to the edge of the part of the stone which is to be removed, and about 1 inch back from this edge. With softer stones and also

76

35. Typical spalls. These show the student sculptor the results he should expect to get with the tools named. Left to right: pitcher work, roughing-out with the heavy point, shaping with the point

as the student gains in experience he can afford to increase these dimensions. Refer to the illustration of the pitcher in position. The operation of the pitcher is in action unlike that of the point or the chisel group and it should be noted that, as I have said above, the pitcher is held perpendicularly to the surface against which it is actually pressed; not at the angle of 40 to 60 degrees as is done with the point or the chisel group. The pitcher is struck a number of times with the heaviest possible swinging blows; exactly opposite to the kind of short stroke tapping which is applied to chisels when finishing. Between blows the working edge of the pitcher is moved a little sideways to and fro on the line; by this I mean on a line which is in continuation of the line of the working edge of the tool itself, side-stepping as it were, in opposite directions. The proud edge of the bevel of the working end should be placed facing inwards.

This process of heavy roughing out with the pitcher is used for as long as possible, taking advantage of the easier yielding tendencies of the natural angles and corners. Obviously, a time arrives when as much work as possible has been done in this way and all this fortuitous advantage has been exploited to the maximum.

36. Showing angle at which chisel should be held; a more acute angle, or in other words, less steep to face of work than with the point. Compare with figure 33 showing work with heavy point. In illustration above the author is seen using a broad chisel for finishing part of surface of an heraldic sculpture in Portland stone

The pitcher has now to be operated on the remaining surfaces which lack the adventitious benefits of the naturally occurring prominences which gave the pitcher a 'bite' on the stone. The way to employ the pitcher on these remaining surfaces is to work it in conjunction with the heavy point. The student must now proceed by first making a small 'chase' in the surface of the stone in a position chosen to take advantage of any prominences there may be. This 'chase' is a half saucer shaped depression about 1 inch to $1\frac{1}{2}$ inches deep with the diametrical boundary in the form of a small face perpendicular to the general surface of the mass of stone. Then place the working end of the pitcher in the 'chase' with its edge against the bottom of the vertical side of the hollow that has just been made to receive it. The tool should be held firmly in the hollow and in position as nearly as possible parallel to the average face of the mass of the stone. The proud edge of the bevel should be inwards. Now strike with swinging, heavy blows of the hammer. A piece of stone of about the size of the palm of the hand should crack off. The size of the spall detached depends, of course, on the hardness of the stone being worked. Repeat the process, methodically working over the whole surface, as much as is necessary.

WORKING WITH THE CLAW

I mentioned earlier that a claw-tool or a claw-bit and holder are alternative tools of which the claw-tool is the more pleasant to use but the claw-bit and holder by far the more economical. It is usually taken up fourth in the sequence—pitcher, heavy point, light point, claw. A matter of personal taste intrudes here: I myself use a claw very little, usually taking the work down far enough with the light point to be able to go straight over to finishing it with the chisel. The majority of sculptors use claw-tools for a great deal of the work. Michelangelo is reputed to have worked extra much with claw-tools and the evidence of his unfinished works seems to confirm this.

The action with the claw-tool is similar to that described for the point, but the spoil produced is, of course, granular rather than the flake-like spalls produced by the point. The purpose of this tool is to remove a layer of stone less thick than that removed by the point but thicker than that taken off by the chisel. It is able to do this because the dents make it 'bite' more deeply than the chisel but at the same time it is prevented from running in unevenly like the point. It can be used more safely when the sculptor is approaching the finished surface than a light point, which may run in here and there rather unpredictably. It produces an almost smooth but furrowed surface which only needs cleaning up with the chisel to finish it.

Michelangelo, who worked so much with the claw, used to go straight over from a fine-toothed claw to finish with rasps and rifflers, and many other sculptors who work mainly in marble have done the same both before and since. Sculpture worked according to this routine manifests a conspicuously characteristic quality arising therefrom. Claw tools were used hardly, if at all, by Romanesque and early medieval sculptors, who used chisels for work which would have been done with either points or claws by sculptors of other periods. This was largely instrumental in producing much of the characteristic quality of their work. I will have more to say on this subject in a later section of the book.

The action of working with point, claw, chisel and gouge is all basically the same. The difference is that, of this range of tools, the point is the one which is held at the steepest, or most obtuse, angle to the surface of the stone, and the chisel and gouge are the ones which are held at the most acute, or least steep, angle; but the student must not make the mistake of thinking that there is a lot of difference between these angles. I wish to emphasize strongly that it should be a universal rule in stone carving that the student must always hammer drive the point, claw, chisel or gouge, never push them at the stone. The only tools that are pushed or rubbed on the surface of the stone are rasps, rifflers, saws and rotating drills. This is a characteristic difference from wood carving in which chisels and gouges are some times pushed at the work.

Gouges are not actually necessary tools. All finishing in sculpture can be perfectly well achieved with the various sizes of chisels, but gouges can sometimes speed up a particular part of the work and so it is handy to have a small selection of them in the studio.

The whole process of sculpture in a wide range of materials, lime-stones, grit-stones and marbles, can be carried out with the use of only these four groups of tools driven with a hammer. To this one must add, providing they are operated with the necessary skill.

However, farther on in the book, I give a supplementary list of tools and an explanation of their use. These are the additional tools that are called for in the working of larger sculptures than have been envisaged in this section of the book. In addition will be found granite tools and their explanation.

CHAPTER SEVEN

BEGINNING A SIMPLE STONE CARVING

The student will find himself confronted with a block of stone which will be either random shaped as quarried, or sawn. The former kind was used for *The Diogenist* as figure 55 shows, and *Singing Negress* (figure 43), and from the latter kind was carved *in situ* the *Sir Edmund Craster*, the block being first fixed in position in the Bodleian Library, and also *The Founder*. In either case first consideration must be given to what is called the natural bedding of the stone. This, which will be dealt with in a later section of the book (page 124), will not be explained here. Having settled the question of what the natural bedding of the stone will permit the next move is to decide how the sculpture ought to be sited within the block to exploit the stone to the best advantage. This is obviously a simple straight forward matter with a sawn block. On the other hand, a random natural shaped block, as quarried, is a challenge to, and an opportunity for the exercise of, the utmost ingenuity. A sawn block provides one with a ready-made flat surface to act as the bed face of the sculpture. The first operation on the random block is to carve this flat surface for a bed face at the place in the block which natural bedding and the other considerations demand.

As the generation of a flat surface from an irregular shape is one of the basic tasks of masonry or sculpture I will deal next with this. As dictated by the design, one may need in forming this flat surface, to take off either a thick layer of stone or the minimum which will clean off all the random cavities and faults in the block. When this has been decided, take up a rule and make a pencil guide line on the stone in the required place. The roughness of the block in the opposing plane at this beginning stage may possibly not permit the rule to lie flat on the block anywhere, but a little common-sense will get over this difficulty. Then take up a heavy point and carve a draft about $\frac{1}{4}$ of an inch above the guide line leaving this as an allowance for heavy-point-work-roughness. A draft is a flat band of surface, conveniently about 1 to 2 inches wide. During these early stages of cleaning up a natural shaped

81

block, the width of a draft is often made to vary by the irregularities of the random shape of the stone in the other plane. The draft must be straight enough from the point of view of the opposing plane, for a rule to be able to stand on its edge on the draft extending the whole length and beyond each side. Another rule is then taken up (it must be long enough to project at least a little at both ends of the block) and held in a suitable position on the opposite side of the block. The student then lowers his eye to the level of the two rules and by trial and alteration gets this second rule on the far side of the block parallel to the one standing on the first draft; a trace from this is then drawn in pencil on the far side of the block. Number two draft is then carved to this line and will be true with number one. When number two is finished, two more drafts are carved joining up the ends of numbers one and two. In effect, the student now has the four edge parts of his required flat surface with an irregular mass of stone standing up all over the middle part. He then lays his rule across the middle of the block from draft to draft and carves a cross draft which lets his rule drop down in until it is touching the two edge drafts. Next he will do this across the other way. He now has four irregular masses of stone separated and surrounded by bands of his potential flat surface. It is now an easy matter to produce the whole flat surface by cleaning off these four irregular prominences. The student must be very cautious not to run in too deep anywhere. If he does so there is no cure but to start again and take the whole face down sufficiently lower to clean off any pits he has made. Furthermore, this can only be done if the block of stone is large enough to allow such latitude. The siting of the sculpture within the block should be so arranged, if circumstances can possibly allow it, that until the heavy roughing out has been carried a long way it can be re-sited to escape natural defects in the stone and minor mistakes. This subject is linked to something that will come up again later. This cutting of drafts is basic to the whole process of the sculptor finding his way about in a block of stone. It is certainly the basis of producing all the geometrical and regular forms. It is only a matter of common-sense to work out from the foregoing routine the corresponding procedure for a curved surface by adding the assistance of templates.

The traditional practice of masons from time immemorial has been based on this procedure of carving drafts set out and governed by rulers and set squares plus the use of templates. This was the routine which shaped the stones which made Chartres and Wells and which, presumably, shaped those of the Parthenon and the Temple of Amenhotep at Luxor as well.

TEMPLATES AND THEIR USE

That important thing the template must now be explained. It is a shape cut out in some stiff sheet material embodying the profile of some part of a piece of masonry or sculpture. It is employed as a try-gauge in tooling down the work. As I have already said in conjunction with the cutting of drafts, the work of masons is based upon the guidance of templates. The design of the templates and the manner in which each one is to be applied in achieving the shape of the stone has to be worked out in relation to the individual case. There is in this the need for, and the opportunity for, the exercise of much ingenuity. Masons usually cut their templates out of sheet zinc. This material is chosen because it is sufficiently strong and hard wearing. At the same time it is fairly easy to cut with tinsmiths' shears. It has the additional advantage of being, of course, non-rusting and sufficiently long lasting. In masons' yards some of the same templates are used time and again on different jobs.

I have adopted the template, this traditional and extensively employed device of the masons, and have extended its use into the sphere of sculpture. The template is a thing that has proved itself by practical application in its traditional association with the craft of stone carving. Developed and applied in the way that I have it provides an aid in the preliminary stages of the work, that can be needed where a sculptor may have to embody, or may choose to embody, a representational element in a certain work. This system of using templates gives him all the practical advantages that can be gained from preliminary model making with none of the extreme undesirableness of that practice from the aesthetic aspect. It avoids completely the danger, inherent in the other practice, of adulterating the qualities of stone carving with the alien kind of forms and rhythms generated in the process of clay modelling.

While the student is at the more elementary level of producing work of the applied art kind he will be using templates as a mason does. They will regulate for him the main shapes. As he progresses to the more advanced stages the use and application of the special kind of life drawings he will be doing and, more particularly, the study of sections taken from the form of the life model, will become obvious. The student having been studying the life model specially from the point of view of the sections through the form, in the manner described in the appropriate part of this book, will be equipped and ready to make the templates he requires. A point of decisive importance is that he must not use this technique of taking sections from the life model and cutting templates to guide his carving as a way of merely copying natural shapes. This misuse of the technique not only could be, but has been, indulged in. It constitutes the great mistake of certain former experimenters on these lines. The purpose of taking sections from the life model is that of study, to cultivate a generous vocabulary of form. On the basis of this vocabulary of form, and understanding of form, he can draw sections from which to make templates in a free manner and in a spirit of creative originality. He will, in fact, be less tempted than otherwise, to lapse into copying the shape of the life model. In relation to the use of templates two aspects of the same tendency assert themselves as the work progresses. The first is that a stage in each work soon arrives at which the significance of the form and of the design *in toto* take control and the use of templates is spontaneously discontinued. The second is that as the sculptor becomes more developed this point arises at an earlier stage in the carving of each work.

As I earlier pointed out masons find zinc sheet the most convenient material from which to make their templates. I find that for the comparatively brief time they need to be used by a sculptor ordinary cardboard is best. Cardboard having a thickness of slightly under $\frac{1}{16}$ inch for small templates, and slightly over for larger ones is convenient. One can draw on it with pencil and short-bladed robust scissors cut it easily. It is a relatively weak material and the student must be careful not to buckle the templates, or to force them, because this is only too easy.

To draw the shape of the templates on the cardboard use tracing paper. Human and animal forms are symmetrical on the model of a duality, to a greater degree than one commonly realizes. The necessary symmetry can be produced in the templates by the simple device of folding and unfolding, along their axial line, the designs made on the tracing paper for the templates.

I again want to stress that in making the drawings on the tracing paper from which to cut the templates the sculptor must look upon his action as one of creative design just as much as at any other stage of the work. This he will do if his study from life model and from other sculptors' work is producing him the right frame of mind. I hold the view that where symmetry occurs in natural forms and is echoed in a work of art the work of art should be made either exactly

84

symmetrical or predeterminedly asymmetrical to a calculated extent as an outcome of the exercise of deliberate choice. I think that it is a fault in a work for it to be asymmetrical to an extent unknown to the sculptor and uncontrolled by the sculptor.

It is a good idea to make the drawings on the tracing paper first to the actual shape that one wants the sculpture to be and then to add the allowance that must be made to compensate for the roughness of the tooling for each stage of the work. About $\frac{1}{2}$ inch should be allowed in templates prepared for heavy point roughing-out; while not much more than $\frac{1}{16}$ inch should be allowed on the templates for finishing with the chisel. Never for sculpture make templates right down to the size and so little as $\frac{1}{16}$ inch allowance will be more used at the masonry level than on sculpture. In sculpture long before one reaches this point the feeling for the thing has taken control and templates have been discarded.

Use templates as little as possible; do not get tied down to them. Their purpose is two-fold. One, to generate and keep exact the form of any purely geometrical-shaped part of the work; for which kind of task their use will be retained by the most experienced sculptor. Two, to give the beginner the necessary minimum of guidance to set him free from the tyranny of clay model copying, with its inherent disadvantage of the debasement of the stone carving through the infiltration of alien influences.

To start off the beginner with the application of templates take, for an example, the simple sandstone trough illustrated on figure 17. For this work, being as it was, no more than a piece of masonry, the following templates were needed: one for the profile of the angled side of the actual trough opening; a second to trace round for the periphery of each of the six duplicate cusped recesses on the sides and ends of the outside of the trough; a third to give the trace for the inside outline of the cusps and a fourth to generate the profile of the set-back of the cusped recesses. Several more minor ones could be of assistance. Of course, the main rectangles of the shape are set out and tested with set-square and rule.

CHAPTER EIGHT

SOME STAGES IN CARVING A SCULPTURE

For up to a few years the sculpture student may continue to find a little daunting the rugged and uncouth prospect presented to him on each first day by the lump of natural rock which is his material.

Unless the stone is to be carved *in situ* and therefore is already fixed on the building, all that has been said in chapter V11 'Beginning a Simple Stone Carving' applies here. I will not repeat it, but refer the reader back. The first stage, therefore, is to carve a bed face on the block in the right position. If the block of stone weighs more than a few hundred-weights this will mean that it will have to be lifted by a chain-tackle into a suitable position to do this work. When this job has been done it will again have to be lifted and turned over and let down on the bed face that has just been carved on it and, incidentally, on which it is likely to rest for the next several hundred years. Next comes the important and decisive task of deciding where, within the block, the different parts of the sculpture should be sited. This can be sketched on the outside of the block with pencil. Then must be decided in what manner the roughing out will be done. In a small sculpture this can best be done, first with the pitcher (the use of which tool has already been described) and following this, the heavy point. In the case of a larger sculpture it may be found that one or more quite large masses of stone have to be removed; pieces having a bulk of several cubic feet. It is very laborious and wasteful of stone simply to carve these away. They can sometimes be split off by the use of plugs and feathers. In this way large blocks of stone can be split off from the parent mass which, in themselves, are sufficient from which to carve other smaller sculptures. Thus both time and valuable stone is saved. However, the greatest care must be taken in this splitting process or, by the crack running the wrong way, the main block may be irretrievably damaged. The technique of splitting by drilling and with plugs and feathers will be gone into later in the book.

For reasons both aesthetic and technical-mechanical, the sculpture should be kept going altogether. By this I mean that all parts, as far as possible, should be kept at the same stage of working; no finishing

37. An early stage in the roughing-out of *The Founder*, an over life-size sculpture (shown in the finished state in figure 2.) Several blocks have been split off with plugs and feathers and more to come (*see* pages 108 ff.) and pitcher work and heavy-point-roughing out is being done with it

of parts here and there while bulk of stone is left elsewhere. The illustrations show a series of stages from block of stone to finished work from the examples of several sculptures and this point, among others, is to be seen in them.

38. A following stage in working *The Founder*. The work is now being done mainly with the light point and chisel

39. *The Diogenist*, a life size figure in Hopton-wood stone (shown finished in position in fig. 3). Here shown at the stage of shaping with the light point. The design of this sculpture involved carving what are for stone, exceptionally free-standing parts to an extent practised mainly by Hellenistic and Renaissance marble carvers. As can be seen here, the technique for this is to leave 'webs' or 'bridges' of stone to support the free-standing parts while they are being carved. When the work is ready for finishing off, these supports are cautiously carved away mainly by drilling and sawing, if the stone is of a kind which will permit this way of working

40. A block of Clipsham stone built into the Bodleian Library, at Oxford, ready for carving *in situ* the portrait sculpture of Sir Edmund Craster. The correct bedding of the stone can clearly be seen in the photograph

41. The roughing-out having been done with points, the sculpture is ready for the carving of the finished form with chisels

42. MARK BATTEN. *Sir Edmund Craster*, the finished portrait. One of the series of hood-moulding terminals, carved *in situ*, in the form of portraits of contemporary officers of the University, on the Bodleian Library, at Oxford

43. Rough, as quarried, block of stone for the *Singing Negress*. The bed surface has been carved and the block then turned over to stand on it.

44. The heavy roughing-out has been done. Note: the work has been kept going all together except for the bottom part, which has been taken one stage more advanced

45. All the roughing-out has been done and the work is now ready for final shaping. The base is again a stage more advanced than the other parts

46. MARK BATTEN. *Singing Negress,* the sculpture finished: it is life-size, in Belgian black marble (see page 122) partly polished and part matt

47. Another in the series of hood-moulding terminals for the Bodleian Library, Oxford, being carved *in situ*. The author is here shown working with the light point having completed the roughing-out stage

The student should tend to hold back on the development of the cavities. This will help to make it possible to re-site the sculpture within the block a little should this be made necessary by natural faults in the stone or slight miscalculations while the work is in the rough state. A very alert watch should be kept on the block in the early stages for signs of defects in the stone.

The sculpture is then taken down with the heavy point, light point, perhaps the claw, and finished off with chisels of various widths, that is if the material is an ordinary limestone or a grit-stone.

Any deep shaped cavities or any piercings running right through parts of the block may have to have a pilot hole if without it they get too difficult to carve. This can be made nowadays with a rotating drill tipped with tungsten carbide. The traditional way of operating a rotating drill was by means of a bow (a bow drill). At the present day it can be operated by means of a convenient geared hand-brace or by electric power. Before the discovery of tungsten carbide for tipping rotating drills a jumper drill, such as is shown in figure 53, had to be used for hard stones like granite.

94

48. MARK BATTEN. *Sir Douglas Veal*, shown opposite being carved, is shown here in the finished state. This is a further one of a series of portraits carved *in situ* on the Bodleian Library at Oxford. They are in the form of hood-moulding terminals carved in Clipsham stone

The appropriate quality for sculptures in limestone is imparted to them by finishing with chisels. This subtly modifies every part of the form to give it a characteristic distinction, not in any sense a mere veneer, but fundamental. It operates long before a chisel is actually used on the work by throwing its influence back before even the roughing out stage, back to the first conception of the design. From the moment the sculptor decides that limestone will be his material and therefore the chisel his finishing tool chisel nuances are in his mind. The quality generated is unique, is strongly characteristic, it has its special value and it cannot be produced, or successfully imitated, by any other process.

Sculptures in marble also, if the natural properties of the material are suitably exploited, have characteristic qualities. Although the tools and the methods of roughing out are largely the same as for ordinary limestone there is a difference in the later stages. Marble character is the outcome of two things. First, that of all stones marble is the strongest in the sense that it will permit the most piercing and undercutting. In other words, it is of all stones the least brittle in relation to its hardness. Second, it is taken up to a finish with either a light point or claw-tools and then the final form is achieved with rasps and rifflers. In most cases it is then polished. This cannot but affect the design at every point.

The extremely hard igneous rocks such as granite and basalt produce a third very characteristic quality in the sculptures made from them. They do so by the reaction upon the sculptor's mind of the methods of working they demand, and the restrictions they impose on the design and character of the forms by their hardness to brittleness ratio. Sculptures in granite are frequently finished by polishing.

The illustrations of complete sculptures will be found grouped mainly according to a classification based on material and technique and not on the more usual historical or racial one. The student should, therefore, refer to these illustrations to supplement the foregoing explanations by the visual experiences which the understanding of any matter of art requires.

CHAPTER NINE

SUPPLEMENTARY LIST OF TOOLS

NEEDED FOR MORE ADVANCED OR LARGER WORKS

GENERAL LIST

A good crowbar about 5 feet long is needed. It can be bought from an ordinary toolshop which sells the larger kinds of tools. The one illustrated in fig. 49 is a specially good one, being made of spring steel by a Cornish granite-toolsmith.

The sculptor needs an ordinary sledge hammer with a head of about 10 to 14 pounds in weight.

He should also have a scabbling hammer or a pick (fig. 50) of which there are several kinds. These usually have to be obtained from businesses which sell tools for quarrying or mining. Scabbling hammers are like sledge hammers with heads of slimmer shape. They usually have an ordinary face peen one end and the other end may be alternatively an obtuse point, a wedge-shape, or a cube with its sharp corners on. The one in the illustration has a wedge shape.

MARBLE TOOLS

The tools described and illustrated in Chapter II under 'Minimum Tool and Material Needs of the Beginner' are, in fact, marble tools. Therefore I need only add to them the tools special to the working of marble and marble-like stones not included before.

First, rasps; these are in appearance similar to those used for general purposes, the dents are a little more widely spaced in proportion to their size, but the main difference is that marble rasps are tempered to a greater degree of hardness. They are only to be obtained from marble masons' or sculptors' tool merchants.

Second, rifflers; these are rather special tools. They are like two small rasps formed on opposite ends of a thin steel bar each end different from the other. The shapes of these miniature rasps come in wide variety, affording great convenience in work. They are ingeniously formed to get into, or around, every imaginable shape of the marble. This can best be understood from figures 51, 52, showing several of them. These tools, again, are only to be bought from sculptors' tool merchants.

49. A useful type of banker (made of oak) for small to medium size works; on the left a scabbling hammer; on the right a sledge hammer and in front a crowbar

POLISHING KIT

This the student will mainly improvise for himself. Polishing is done with pads impregnated with fine abrasives of various kinds and degrees of fineness. Felt pads are used by the masonry trade but

50. Demonstrating the use of a scabbling pick. Shown are Greek masons heavy-roughing-out Pentelic marble in a quarry on Mount Pentelikon. This is one of the original quarries first used in Classical times for the building and the sculpture of the Parthenon which has been brought into use again for restoration of the Parthenon

nylon rags are good. The first stages of polishing are smoothing processes in which the abrasive is usually finely powdered carborundum or emery. For the final polish several materials are used and there are many individually held opinions on the subject. It is generally done with what is called masons' putty powder, which is usually composed of finely powdered oxide of zinc or oxide of tin or a mixture of the two. Some sculptors use rouge at one stage. In polishing sculpture something which has been produced for industrial purposes will be found very useful. This is a kind of abrasive coated paper which is water-resistant and is sometimes called Wet-or-Dry, or, alternatively, waterproof carborundum paper. It is manufactured

99

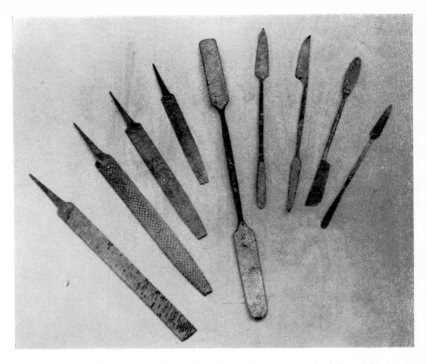

51. A selection of rasps and rifflers, those for softer stone on the left and for harder stone and marble on the right

in a greater variety of finenesses than is needed even for sculpture polishing. By working down through the grades at reasonable intervals it will be found to give very good results for every stage except the final polish. All this work of rubbing down and polishing is done with plenty of water in the trade and by most sculptors. I have not found it essential to use water with the abrasives or the putty powder, nor have I found it always convenient.

Among the illustrations the reader will find several Ancient Egyptian and Central American polished sculptures and the *Singing Negress* by the author. In the *Singing Negress* polished parts are counterbalanced in harmony with matt portions.

I will here point out that the very high gloss produced on marble and some other stones by the masonry trade is obtained improperly by using acid to melt, as it were, the surface of the marble or stone. The gloss obtained in this way has a relatively short life and is therefore inferior to a good friction-and-abrasive polish. There is,

100

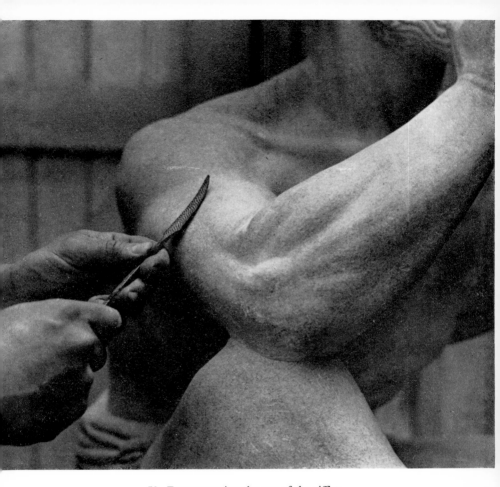

52. Demonstrating the use of the riffler

in addition, a long-term danger that some of the acid may have been absorbed by the stone.

GRANITE TOOLS

In a very general sense granite tools work on the same principles as stone or marble tools but there is a fundamental difference. It is that while hardened tempered steel is harder than the substance of both limestone and marble, it is actually softer than the minerals composing most of the crystals of which granite or other igneous rocks are formed. This determines that the granite group of stones cannot be cut, sawn, rasped or riffled by means of tools made of steel. Steel tools

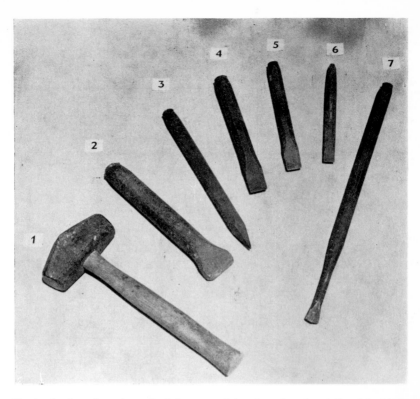

53. A selection of granite tools: 1, hammer; 2, hand set; 3, point; 4, 5 and 6, chisels;
7, jumper drill

can only work granite by exploiting the one quality which the steel
has, that of being tougher than the stone, although it is less hard.
This means that all the group of rasps, rifflers, saws and rotating drills
are automatically ruled out as being impotent against the granite. The
only kind of steel tools, therefore, that can be employed on granite,
are the hammer-driven group which either split off or powder away
the stone by breaking down the cohesion between the crystals of
which it is composed.

Granite hammers, as the outcome of these determining factors, are
heavier in the head than marble hammers and the heads are made of
cast steel. Also the handles are longer in proportion, as a more
powerful and therefore swinging blow has to be used, and are also
comparatively slim and slightly springy, which granite masons say
reduces the fatigue of this very heavy work.

102

The butt ends of all granite tools are a truncated shape like an ordinary cold chisel. Another group feature characterizing them is that they are forged from a much thicker steel bar than the corresponding stone or marble tools; furthermore, they are much more robust, heavier and more obtuse in the shape of their working ends.

The *hand-set* is a tool which operates on the same principle as does a pitcher for stone or marble and has a working end of similar shape. For granite there is a variation by which the rectangular working face of some of these tools is at right angles to the body, not bevelled. The hand set is much longer in the body than the pitcher and far more robust as can be seen from the illustration.

The *granite point*, in shape, is governed by the general characteristics set out above.

The *granite chisel*, of which three sizes are shown in the illustration, has, again, the same general characteristics.

In place of the rifflers used for marble, slips of carborundum are used for granite. The ordinary tool-merchants' cigar-shaped carborundum 'scythe-stone' in a worn-out condition is very convenient for this work. Broken and worn-down ones should be collected. The new ones are rather too large and obtuse.

The *polishing* of granite sculpture is done with pads impregnated with carborundum powder of varying grades down to the finest for finishing. This powder is a commercial product which is widely and easily obtainable. The waterproof paper, 'Wet-or-Dry', coated with carborundum abrasive mentioned in connection with marble polishing is equally effective for this purpose. It is made in many grades, down to extremely fine.

In connection with granite carving tungsten carbide must again be mentioned. This is a newly discovered material, like a metal, but having great hardness, greater even than granite. It is used for tipping rotating drills with which granite can be drilled. Also chisel-type tools are made with tungsten carbide tips inserted into steel bodies. These stand up quite well to granite carving; they have disadvantages which make them far from perfect, but if the student works in granite he should try them.

TOOLS FOR SPLITTING STONE

Stone-wedges are the simplest and most elementary and anciently used device for splitting stone. They are not unlike ordinary wood-splitting wedges but are more robust and of better steel. They are usually about 6 inches long by 2 inches-plus wide and one is shown in

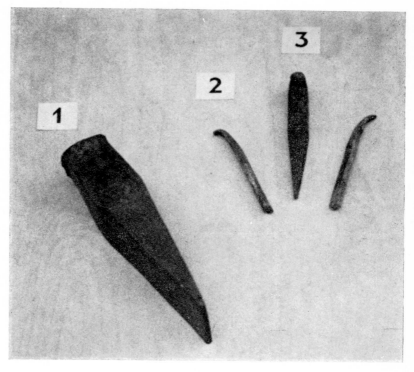

54. Tools for stone splitting: 1, stone wedge; 2, feather, used in pairs in conjunction with; 3, a plug

the illustration. They are used for rough work on the softer kinds of limestones and sandstones.

Plugs and feathers are important and indispensable tools for splitting granite and other tough stones. Each unit consists of three parts, a plug and a pair of feathers. The necessary niceties of their shape the student will see when he examines them. A feather (feathers work in pairs) consists of a piece of steel about 3 inches $\times$ $\frac{1}{2}$ inch. In cross-section it is almost semicircular except at one end where it is forged into a slightly hooked shape. Between a pair of these, assembled flat face inwards, goes the plug. The plug is a small steel wedge specially made of the appropriate size and shape. These three add up to an expanding cylindrical shape. For splitting stone a sculptor needs about 8 to 12 of these units. They can only be bought from granite masons' and some sculptors' tool-merchants.

Drills are associated tools in the process of stone splitting. There are two types, the old traditional jumper-drill and the rotating drill. Until modern times jumper-drills were the only ones that could be used on granites and grit-stones. The introduction of tungsten carbide tipped twisted-flute drills has changed this. The jumper-drill is used with a hammer and rotated slightly between blows. One is shown (fig. 53) in the illustration of granite tools. In Renaissance times the bow drill was used on marble to make a line of very closely spaced small holes in preparation for splitting the stone. The bow drill is only suitable for making a hole of small diameter. In preparing to split stone with plugs and feathers the sculptor needs one long tungsten carbide tipped drill, about 12 inches long, with a diameter of, say, ⅝ inch. He also needs a drill of larger diameter which need not be longer than about 5 inches. The exact diameter of this drill cannot be decided upon until after the sculptor has got his plugs and feathers, because the size must be exactly right to suit the size of the plugs and feathers. To decide this, assemble a plug and feather unit in its contracted position. Then take a pair of callipers and measure the diameter of the circle which is made by the outside surfaces of the feathers. This is the diameter for the short drill. If the sculptor is going to use jumper drills the same applies. The rotating drills can conveniently be operated by an ordinary geared hand-brace.

To remove the main bulk of stone surrounding a sculpture by splitting off, sawing is often a part of the preparation. The old traditional type of stone saw is called a *grub saw* and is like a large two-handled (two man) wood-saw. The difference is that it has no teeth but a slightly wavy edge. It is drawn to and fro by two men and a mixture of sharp sand and water is fed into the cut with a ladle. More recently the sand has been replaced with hard steel granules called 'shot'. Granites could not be sawn with this tool. Softer limestones are sometimes cut with a saw very similar to a large wood saw with coarse teeth which are not 'set'. I myself have found that with the modern improvement in steels a saw produced commercially for the everyday purpose of cutting firewood works as well as any other for those stones which can be sawn in this sort of way. This is the largest size of frame saw, of the kind with a renewable blade and a tubular spring frame, commonly called a 'woodman'. It is a useful and economical discovery as the replacement blades, being mass produced, are relatively cheap. The frame of the largest size will allow the saw to run into the stone to a useful depth.

CHAPTER TEN

GRANITE CARVING
AND STONE SPLITTING

I have combined granite carving and stone splitting because, while splitting technique has its application with all kinds of stone, it plays a proportionately far larger part in the working of granite. Until the introduction in modern times of machinery having rotating disc saws, edged with industrial diamonds or carborundum, splitting was the only way of doing the major work on granite. For the individual sculptor in his own studio splitting remains the only practicable way of removing large masses of granite.

Certain characteristic properties of granite as distinct from other kinds of stone determine the different way in which it is worked. These are that while most of the minerals of which it is composed are harder than any steel the cohesion between the crystals is not proportionately so great. In other words it is very much harder but not proportionately more difficult to split.

In practice this means that the sculptor will find that the heavy point with which he can rip into limestone or marble is useless for removing bulk of granite. The removal of all but that which is required by the detailed shaping has to be done with the hand-set. This tool, as has been mentioned above, corresponds to the pitcher for working limestone and the instructions for working with the pitcher will apply here for the hand-set. The obvious difference is that correspondingly smaller spalls will be removed unless far more force is applied. The illustration (fig. 10) of a granite masons' yard includes a team of two men working with a set and a sledge-hammer which is, of course, a more powerful exploitation of the same principles. As with other stones the next tool is the heavy point and it should be noted that no light point is used on granite.

In working granite the heavy point has to be held at a steeper or more obtuse angle to the stone than it would be on marble or limestone.

The student might well wonder why the granite point and chisel are so much bulkier and heavier than those for marble and think that this may result in loss of the efficiency of the blow. This is

55. MARK BATTEN. *The Diogenist*, sculpture in Hopton-wood stone (shown finished and in position in figure 3). To demonstrate how the stone-splitting technique is used to advance the early stages of the carving, the sculpture is here shown with photographs of the actual blocks of stone which were split off. The three blocks are shown in positions slightly drawn back from the positions they were in when still parts of the original block

56. A split block, its face affording a sectional view of the work. Note: the long twisted-flute drill for the pilot holes; the short drill for sizing holes to take the plug and feathers; the plug and feathers, top right, are turned out of working position to show them in the photograph; notice also how true the pilot holes have been drilled—a secret of successful stone cleaving

not so. I want again to emphasize that experience has evolved the right shape and weight for these tools. A tool as light as a marble or stone tool put at the steep angle and struck with the necessary force at the unyielding granite does what stone masons call 'shivers'. It rebounds from the granite with a violent vibration which stings the palm of the hand.

After the heavy point come the two main sizes of chisel with the small one for special places; all much more obtuse at their working ends and more robust then marble tools; also used at a steeper angle. Chisels do a lot of the work on granite but they do not split off spalls; they only remove a kind of granules or very coarse powder.

The final smooth shape is produced by rubbing down with slips of carborundum. These slips of carborundum quickly wear away

108

57. Showing the second stage of the technique of splitting stone with 'plugs' and 'feathers' on the scale used by quarrymen. The latter are seen inserting the 'plugs' and 'feathers' in the holes. See figure 56. (Courtesy Bath and Portland Group Ltd.)

and by using them and laying them on one side, with a little ingenuity one can cultivate a useful selection suitable for every part of the work.

The sculptor will find that because the steel cannot cut the granite and therefore the carving has to be a violent breaking process, the granite has to be treated as relatively vastly more brittle than stone or marble (although it is, of course, actually very much stronger than these). It will not permit free-standing parts nor undercutting except where there is plenty of bulk. Even a design involving the connection of two bulky parts by a rather thin waist of stone is hardly possible. Commercial granite masons required to make things like the conventional poppy-head architectural ornament often have as many as one in two breakages. The student will notice that the Ancient Egyptians, who were very experienced granite carvers, usually took the precaution of reinforcing the necks of their figures in granite by designing the ingenious addition of some headdress or similar support.

When working granite the amount of tool grinding and fire-sharpening is vastly greater than with stone or marble and makes a laborious addition to the work.

The next subject is the important one of stone splitting. The natural fact of which this process takes advantage is that stone has not nearly such great strength in tension as it has in compression. The great power of hammer-driven wedges is brought to bear on this lesser tensile resistance of the stone.

Splitting, which gives such profitable results, has to be very thoughtfully planned to get the desired effect and to avoid disasters. The first practical point is that it is not possible to make a crack 'run' other than in one plane and direction and as straight as it will. In other words, if an 'L'-shaped detaching is needed the short leg of the 'L' has got to be opened up first by cutting a chase, or by sawing, or usually by combining both to conserve labour. Then the long leg of the 'L' can be made to 'run' as a crack. When the necessary preparation has been made and the piece to be cracked off has been freed of stone all round, the line of the desired crack should be drawn in pencil on the block. Consideration has to be given to the grain of the stone, the direction of the bedding, and everything else known about the block, such as natural faults. Then the position of the holes has to be decided upon, how far apart and from which faces to drill. It is a question of judgment, of striking a balance between precaution and economy of labour. The illustration (fig 56) of this kind of work shows a good average fracture in Hopton-wood stone, a fairly large one. From this the reader can clearly see how the holes should be sited to

58. Showing stone splitting with plugs and feathers; working at the very large scale on which the method is employed for the extraction of stone in quarries. Stage three: driving the plugs. This is one of the renowned limestone quarries at Portland (*see* page 120). Only the scale is different, the method the same, when employed for roughing out a sculpture (Courtesy Bath and Portland Group Ltd.)

get the best effect. If the sculptor is working on a valuable piece of stone, or on one that has already had valuable work done on it, it is wise to take an extra precaution which is not always taken, or, in fact, known about. This is well shown in the illustration. Pilot holes are drilled deeply into the block on the line of the intended fracture with a drill not quite so large as that required for the plug and feather unit. It is most important to drill these pilot holes very true on the line or their effect is wasted or may even do more harm than good. The illustration shows how accurate were those in the example. The outer 4 inches or so of each hole is bored out with the larger diameter drill to the size required for the plug and feather unit. When all is ready the plug and feather units are assembled and inserted in the prepared holes. In placing the plugs and feathers in position it should be realized that those shown in the illustration have had to be rotated through one right angle out of their correct working position in order to show them in the photograph. While as a general principle oil or grease should be kept as far as possible from stone, it is helpful to grease very sparingly the metal to metal faces of the plugs and feathers. When they have been arranged in the correct position the plugs are lightly tapped to make them 'grip'. It is only too easy to let the plugs or feathers slip down into the holes and lose them. When the other preparations have been made something suitable should be arranged to catch the piece of stone as it jumps off. It will do so instantaneously and without warning. Even the main block may overbalance when the change of centre of gravity takes place so suddenly and precautions should be taken against the chance of injury to the sculptor or assistant or to either piece of stone.

When all the plugs and feathers are in position and 'gripping' they are struck first with a hand hammer, each in turn following a routine. The force of the hammer blows is gradually increased up to a sledge-hammer blow. Watch the job carefully and do not step up the force of the hammer blows unevenly or impatiently. After a length of time usually anything between 10 to 20 minutes the note of the hammering that echoes from the stone goes 'dead' and suddenly the piece of stone jumps off. In that moment you see your job done or, if the planning was wrong, your block very likely damaged beyond use.

In the illustration showing the granite mason's yard (fig. 10) the end of the block being point worked shows the way in which it has been split with plugs and feathers. The point to observe is that, as it is still only a rough block, the rough and ready yard standards of work

59. Showing how efficient is the 'plug' and 'feather' method of splitting stone. The process is here to be seen expertly completed by Portland quarrymen (Courtesy Bath and Portland Group Ltd.)

were used. No pilot holes were drilled and that it was only drilled and 'plugged' working from one face, the top.

Of sculptures by the author illustrated in this book two were worked by the above technique. *The Diogenist* (figs. 3, 39, 55) in its early stages had one large and two smaller blocks split off; one at the front and one at each side of the head. *The Founder* (figs. 2, 37, 38) had the same number; one in front of the head, and one on each side below the arms.

CHAPTER ELEVEN

ESSENTIAL PRACTICAL KNOWLEDGE ABOUT STONE

The student and the sculptor get their supply of stone alternatively from a mason's yard or from a stone merchant (these two are often combined) or direct from the quarry. The reader may discover that, to his great advantage, he happens to live in stone country; on the other hand, he may have to obtain his stone from some distance away.

Undoubtedly the ideal thing to do, for several reasons, is to visit the quarry selected and choose and buy the stone on the spot and arrange for its transport to the studio. One advantage of this procedure is the saving of money. Another is the chance it gives to select a better and more suitable piece of stone. A third is the useful knowledge about the particular kind of stone to be gained by examining it at the quarry face, and discussing it with the foreman of the scappling yard. If quarrymen can be induced to talk they usually have useful knowledge about their own particular stone.

On the other hand, it is safer for the beginner to buy a selected block from a mason or merchant. Do not neglect the possibility that the merchant may have a bargain, an odd piece left over from a job that would be quite suitable for your needs. Another possibility the student should explore is that there may be in his neighbourhood odd pieces of stone lying about to be had for the asking. This particularly applies in stone country. Furthermore, if he lives in stone country he may, when he has acquired some experience, do his own quarrying where rocks are naturally exposed in cliffs or other outcrops.

In Europe, which has been thickly populated for thousands of years, one may, unfortunately, be fairly sure that all the specially desirable stones have already been discovered and exploited. By contrast, sculptors working in such countries as the U.S.A., Australia, South Africa, or New Zealand, are specially fortunate in the exciting chance they have of discovering in their own neighbourhood, or even on their own land, hitherto unknown stones of beautiful colour and texture. Before they can expect to do this they must, of course, have gained the necessary experience to be able to judge a stone's qualities.

The essential basis for understanding stone depends on having a proper mental picture of the main classifications. I find many students and even sculptors confused by a chaotic mental picture of a multitude of stones each a little different from the next and falling into no groups.

Stones fall into the following classification: first, igneous rocks; second, sedimentary rocks; third, metamorphic rocks. Igneous rocks are those which have been formed by solidification through cooling of the primeval rock magma of which the world is composed; the original rocks. Sedimentary rocks are those formed from the products of the disintegration of the original rocks by their reconsolidation, during vast ages of geological time, into new rocks. Metamorphic rocks are those formed from sedimentary rocks by a change made in their nature caused by the heat and pressure upon them of geological disturbances such as volcanic eruptions.

IGNEOUS ROCKS	SEDIMENTARY ROCKS	METAMORPHIC ROCKS
Granites	Sandstones or grit-stones	Marbles
Gabbros	Limestones	Serpentines
Basalts	Magnesian limestones	Steatite
	(called dolomitic)	Slates

Although it is true that there is a large number of minerals contained in small proportions in stone, the main bulk of most stones is made up of one or more of a comparatively small number of substances. These few fundamental mineral substances produce the main characteristics of the stones. The many others present in small quantities usually contribute the variations in colour between one variety and another.

These fundamental substances are the oxides of the metals silicon, aluminium, calcium and magnesium. These are known respectively as silica, alumina, lime and oxide of magnesium (almost always found in combination with other substances as dolomite). These substances in various combinations and with carbon dioxide form most of the bulk of the different kinds of stone. All this leads to a simple practical classification as follows)—

    A.   Granites, gabbros (black granite) and basalt

    B.   Sandstones (sometimes called grit-stones)

C. Limestones and magnesian limestones (called dolomites)
D. Marbles
E. Serpentine, steatite, alabaster and slate

A. GRANITE AND OTHER IGNEOUS STONES

This group comprises the hardest-to-carve stones and among them the most durable ones. Granites, on the average, are about ten times as strong and resistant to carving as limestones. The chemical composition of most of the igneous stones is generally more complicated than the others. Granite is mainly a mixture of the crystals of felspar, silica and mica welded together. Of this mixture the silica and the felspar are harder than steel. What is known as black granite is called by geologists gabbro (see above). Basalt is a black igneous rock which occasionally has been used by sculptors. The great advantages of these stones are their strength and durability and the good polish they take. The disadvantages, the great difficulty of working them and the unpleasant black and white, or other speckled, appearance of the paler coloured ones. They have a wide range of colour but all the paler ones are speckled; light grey, dark grey, to black; pink, up to dark brownish red; dark greyish green. The darker coloured and the black varieties are very attractive materials.

Granites, in variety, occur in most parts of the world. In Britain they are to be found mainly in Cornwall, Devon, Wales, Cumberland and northern Scotland, where they are extensively quarried around Aberdeen. In Cornwall, the other great granite district, the stone is brought down from the various quarries up on the moor to the little port of Penryn to be worked and shipped from there.

In other parts of Europe, Norway, Sweden and Finland are prolific sources. Sweden and Finland both produce a very good black granite. French granite, mostly speckled grey, mainly comes from Brittany.

The U.S.A. has good supplies of granite mainly in two regions. First, the mountainous area in the eastern states called the Appalachian region running from Maine and Vermont in the north to Georgia in the south. Throughout this area granite quarries will be found notably at Barre in Vermont and a very large number in Maine of which Vinalhaven, Jonesport, and Crotch Island are well known. Moving south, quarries will be found at Bradford and Waterford in Connecticut; at Plompton Junction in New Jersey; at Gettysburg and near Philadelphia in Pennsylvania; at Salisbury, North Carolina;

at Winnsborough, South Carolina; and at Stone Mountain near Atlanta in Georgia. The second region is the Rocky Mountain area in the States of Idaho, Montana, Colorado, New Mexico and down to Texas at Granite Mountain in Burnett County. Granite extends also into California and is quarried as well in Wisconsin.

Australia has an abundance of granite in almost all parts. In New South Wales there are well-known quarries of red granites at Cape How and Barren Jack. The usual black and white mottled variety comes from near Moruya in Dampier County. Green varieties come from Bowral about 85 miles from Sydney. Victoria has vast supplies of granite and there are well-known quarries at Bendigo and a good red variety comes from Gabo Island.

In New Zealand's North Island granite is quarried at Mohan in Coromandel County and at other places. In the South Island much granite is quarried at Ruapuke Island. New Zealand has also much good black basalt, a very attractive material but extremely hard.

There are large quantities of granite near most of the chief cities of South Africa, but quarries are not numerous. There is one near Pretoria called Pyramid Quarry. Near Cape Town there is Allens Quarry in the Paarl Mountains and the Higgo Quarry in the French Hoek valley.

In ancient times the Egyptians made much sculpture in granite and some extremely fine examples are included among the end plates. They were able to do this granite and basalt carving as long as six thousand years ago and were the first people in the world to do so, as far as we know.

B. SANDSTONES (SOMETIMES CALLED GRIT-STONES)

These stones are composed of grains of the mineral substance silica stuck together. In some kinds, grains of silica, originally separate, have been stuck together by the action of a vast pressure in the presence of water and often also heat so that they have become welded together without the cementing action of any other substance. In others, the grains of silica are cemented together by a matrix of calcium carbonate or alternatively by oxide of iron, or a mixture containing these. The silica itself is one of the most enduring and indestructible substances in the world. Sand, which is grains of silica, is formed when the other constituents of igneous rocks, such as granite, decompose shedding the silica in an unchanged condition. This illustrates the durability of silica. Sandstones or grit-stones composed of as high as 98% of silica are the most enduring stones in the world,

118

more so even than granite, being, as they are, of the type in which the grains are welded together by heat and pressure (this is the kind of sandstone usually distinguished as a grit-stone). They only decay if fixed in an unsuitable juxtaposition to limestone and for a reason that there is not space to go into in this book. The other kind of sandstones in which the grains of silica are cemented by a matric of calcium carbonate or of iron oxide have only about the same weathering resistance as limestones because they are dependent on this cementing power of the calcium carbonate or of the iron oxide. As mentioned earlier in the book grit-stones are very laborious to work because the silica is harder than steel. They have the further disadvantage that the dust is very bad for the sculptor's lungs, tending to bring on silicosis. Against this, some of them are among the most durable materials in the world. Sandstones cannot be polished.

In Britain the best sandstones are to be found occurring in a broad band running roughly south to north through the middle of the country from the Bristol Channel area to the neighbourhood of Edinburgh, with quarries in all parts of it. There are famous varieties at the south end near Bristol such as Blue Pennant; in the Midlands there are many quarries in the Darley Dale area and into Nottinghamshire with its Red Mansfield and White Mansfield. Yorkshire has many quarries, including what is called York Stone (suitable for flagstones but not sculpture). The best of the grit-stones are to be found at the north end of the belt near Edinburgh, in for instance, the Craigleith and Hailes quarries (the former now closed down).

Of the countries with which we are mainly concerned outside Britain the best sandstones are most abundant in the U.S.A., Australia and South Africa.

In the U.S.A. the good sandstones are mainly found in the area of the Middle Western Plains, particularly in the north of this area in the neighbourhood of the Great Lakes. Two good examples in Minnesota are the Kettle River quarries and the Cofax quarries in Dunn County which yield a stone good for sculpture. In Ohio in Cuyahoga County there are the Euclid Bluestone quarries. On the Pacific side of the States in California in Colusa County a greenish-grey fine-grained stone is obtained from the Sites quarries.

In Australia in the State of Victoria a good sandstone of a soft dove grey and suitable for sculpture is quarried near Stawell in the Grampian Hills. In New South Wales the city of Sydney is built over a good sandstone called Hawkesbury, of which there are many quarries, Hunter's Hill and Pyrmont being well known. There are, no doubt, many other sandstones in Australia that could be, and are being, developed.

South Africa's Table Mountain is a source of sandstone but it is of a greater hardness than most sculptors, certainly beginners, would care to tackle. Natal has quarries, the Rosetta and the Ecca, which provide a good sandstone of a kind more suitable for sculpture.

C. LIMESTONES AND MAGNESIAN LIMESTONES

Limestones are composed of calcium carbonate and dolomitic limestones of a double carbonate of calcium and magnesium. Both of these are pure white unless stained by other minerals. The commonest staining agents are oxides of iron. For practical purposes these two stones may be considered as having very similar qualities, there being only slight relative differences in weathering behaviour, upon which I shall not dwell. Many limestones contain fossilized shells and marine creatures' skeletons to the point that some of them are almost entirely composed of the remains of marine life.

Many more of the world's sculptures are carved in some form of limestone than in any other kind of stone. From the point of view of working, limestones respond to carving by steel tools better than any other kind of stone. Unfortunately, they are not quite so durable as the best grit-stones or granite. In spite of this, they are so highly desirable from the point of view of working, that not only most of the world's sculptures but also the majority of the world's stone buildings are made of them. The more dense and harder limestones take an attractive, but not super-gloss polish.

In Britain the main limestones lie in a broad belt extending in a south-westerly to north-easterly direction, obliquely across England from the Isle of Portland at one end to the Humber Estuary at the other; almost alongside, and to the east of, the belt of sandstones. All the way along this broad band occur quarries yielding stone basically the same but having slight variations in texture, colour, hardness and durability. At the southern end we have the quarries of the world-famous Portland Stone, farther north Bath Stone, then the stones of Oxfordshire and the Cotswolds, then in Rutland the well-known Clipsham Stone and following the belt farther north-east we have the quarries of Lincolnshire, such as Ancaster. The more northerly and westerly side of this belt has the harder and more dense limestones which take a good polish and are like marbles, although not, strictly speaking, marbles. They occur to the west of the belt in Devonshire round Torquay and mainly in Derbyshire, from which comes Hopton-wood and Hadene.

In the countries other than Britain many have good supplies of limestones, notably, France, Belgium, Italy, Greece, the U.S.A.

In France the main limestone belt runs roughly north to south through the middle of the country. Starting at the northern end we have the famous quarries at Caen in Normandy. A good many quarries occur all along the belt, each serving its district until the belt ends in the Alpes-Maritimes at the Mediterranean Coast.

In Belgium the so-called Petit Granit is really a dense hard limestone stretching in a band east to west through the country with many quarries.

Italy's Appenines have many limestone quarries on their western slopes. Near Rome the famous Travertine has been quarried and used for over two thousand years and at present is taken from the Tivoli and Sabino quarries. When freshly got out it is very soft and easy to work, but it hardens very much on exposure and lasts quite well. Another well-known Italian limestone is Istrian Stone, which is dense and takes a good polish. It is a warm grey colour similar to British Hopton-wood and Hadene. It has been used for a very long time. There are quarries at San Stefano and Nabresina.

The U.S.A. has abundant deposits of limestone, mainly in the states of Indiana, Iowa and Kentucky. In Indiana there is a well-known quarry at Bedford in Lawrence County producing a good stone for sculpture. In Kentucky there is one near Memphis Junction. The limestone spreads through other states, mainly those of the more eastern part of the central plain and there are quarries in many parts of this district.

In Australia limestones are found on the eastern flanks of the mountains in Queensland and transported to Brisbane. In Victoria the Waurn Ponds quarries produce a yellowish medium-grained stone.

New Zealand's South Island has Oamaru Stone from Otago, a rather soft limestone but quite suitable for sculpture.

D AND E. MARBLES AND OTHER METAMORPHIC ROCKS

Metamorphic rocks, which include the marbles, were rocks, mainly sedimentary ones, that after being deposited have undergone a chemical change under the influence of heat and pressure, usually from volcanic action. Of these the various marbles form, for sculpture, the most important group. They provide the sculptor with a material reasonably easy to work, taking a good polish, and giving an abundant range of colours and coloured veinings. They have been a favoured material for thousands of years. Most of the sculpture of the Classical and of the Renaissance periods was carved in marble.

Britain unfortunately has no true marble although, as has already been mentioned, some limestones from Derbyshire and Devonshire and from the Isle of Purbeck, Dorset, take a good polish and are somewhat similar to marble in their properties. Alabaster is found mainly in Derbyshire, at Chellaston Quarries, but it must not be forgotten that alabaster will not stand out-of-doors so that its use is very limited. England has some other metamorphic rocks, namely, the serpentine of the Lizard district of Cornwall (which is hardly used at all by sculptors) and, also in Cornwall, the Polyfant Stone from near Launceston. This is a very attractive dark-grey stone but unfortunately not very durable.

Those parts of the world best provided with marble are the northern shores of the Mediterranean and the U.S.A.

Italy is the present source of white marble in Europe, with its famous quarries at Carrara. It also has a large variety of plain coloured and of veined marbles situated in different parts of the country.

Greece and the Greek Islands are the most ancient and famous source of marbles both white and coloured. The marble from Pentelikon has been used for thousands of years and its beauty is due to it being very slightly stained from pure white to a creamy shade by minute traces of iron oxide. Parian is another equally well-known Greek white marble. The island of Tinos yields a beautiful varigated green marble and the Island of Euboea a green-veined one called Cipollino.

Belgium has one of the finest black marbles in the world, known to have been quarried at Mazy, near Namur, for nearly a thousand years.

The U.S.A. has many marble quarries throughout the Appalachian region, but mainly in New England. The chief area is in the State of Vermont and running down into New York State. Vermont has too many marble quarries to list, giving mainly white and green, or green-veined, varieties. The quarries are mostly situated on the west slopes of the Green Mountains in that State. In New York State, Dutchess County, at South Dover, a white marble is quarried; and black marble at Glens Falls and at Plattsburgh. The other State with the most marble is Tennessee, in the area of Knoxville. There are also some marbles quarried in California in Tuolumne County at the Columbia Quarries, and in Bernardino County at Victor and Barstow.

60. A limestone quarry, one of the famous group on the Isle of Portland. This abundant source of good stone was first exploited for use outside its own area for the rebuilding of London after the Great Fire of 1666, St. Paul's Cathedral being one example of its use at that time. Today the quarries are still as busy (Courtesy Bath and Portland Group Ltd.)

Australia has a wealth of marble mainly unexploited, but quarries exist in New South Wales, Queensland, Victoria and South Australia. Some well-known ones are Fernbrook, New South Wales; Rockhampton, Queensland; Gippsland, Victoria; Angaston and Macclesfield in South Australia.

Steatite, or soapstone, is very soft, greyish in colour, with a pleasant appearance, and comes mainly from Central Africa.

THE BEDDING OF SEDIMENTARY ROCKS: FREESTONES

This is the explanation of a subject that has been referred to earlier in the book. Sedimentary rocks, as their name implies, are rocks which have been formed from deposits of the disintegration products of primary rocks. They have been laid down on the beds of seas or lakes in the vastly ancient times of the geological past. They have been reconsolidated into new stones. This has given to most of them a stratified structure. Stones of this type are said to have a bedding plane; all the others without this are called the freestones.

Those sedimentary rocks which have this laminated grain running through them must have the fullest consideration given to their grain in the design of the sculpture. A general rule both for stone used in sculpture and for that used in building, is to keep the stone on its natural bed, that is the horizontal bedding planes of the stone in a horizontal plane in the sculpture. When the sculptor is experienced he will be able to decide what to do in special cases. All this is a matter of decisive importance for the durability of the sculpture. The necessity for the correct bedding of stone creates difficult practical problems, one of which is that of dealing with quarrymen, who are often unscrupulous when faced with the extravagance in stone that correct bedding sometimes involves. Ignorance of, or neglect of, this vital precaution has led to certain works decaying even during the lifetime of their sculptor.

The freestones are, happily, without this inconvenient prohibition. They constitute the igneous rocks, the metamorphic rocks and some of the limestones, mainly the more dense and marble-like ones. The great advantage which freestones have is that blocks of it can be turned into any position in which their shape best suits the shapes of the projected sculpture with no loss of durability.

A powerful magnifying glass of about 10X for studying the grain of stone, is a thing the student should get.

61. General view of a quarry on Mount Pentelikon in Greece (see also figure 50). Pentelic marble
is here seen being quarried for the present partial restoration of the Parthenon in Athens. This
was one of the original quarries from which the stone was taken in Classical times for the sculpture and for the building of the Parthenon. It has been re-opened and extended. Here the stone
is seen being quarried by the traditional methods by hand with almost no mechanisation and with
minimal, or without use of explosives. Where enough labour is available this produces stone in
a much more sound and reliable condition for sculpture. There is also far less general wastage
of stone

125

PLATES

SECTION ONE

Hard, relatively brittle and mostly polishable stones

The unusual way in which the plates are grouped in this book is the outcome of their being considered from the point of view of a practising stone carver. It is more usual to find such illustrations arranged according to the sort of grouping which historical or racial considerations would seem to dictate. As I have said earlier in this book the meaning and appeal of a work of art cuts right across the divisions of language, civilization, race and time. It is manifest that art is the product of something which some people in all communities have in common. Not only does this community within communities universally appreciate, but they universally react with great similarity under similar conditions. In this field of the fine arts the outstanding manifestation of affinity is between sculptors responding to, for instance, a hard polished stone, rather than that springing from community of race, religion or period. Influences originating in technique and material play far more decisive parts in the formation of style than seems generally to be realized. The compelling action of these agencies is obvious to all who actually practice the arts, but not unnaturally tends to be greatly underestimated by the critic or art historian, who, of course, is not under the constant impact, as the artist is, of these more than guiding influences. Examination of the plates as they are here arranged will argue my point far more persuasively than can words. For instance, the reader cannot fail to be struck by the remarkable affinity of feeling shown between the early Central American half-length figure from Honduras, executed in a soft limestone, and some of the European Romanesque sculptures executed in a similar material, although by artists whose civilization, race and religion had nothing in common. Again, notice how the reaction between material and a certain universal element running through all mankind produces a striking similarity of feeling between the Ancient Egyptian sculptures in granite and the Ancient Mexican ritual mask and also the figure from Easter Island.

The plates will be found arranged in three groups. The first group, immediately following, is of those sculptures which are the outcome of the artists' response to a hard and relatively brittle and (in most cases) polishable stone. Elements universally present in man responding to the dictates of the material produce certain qualities of style whether they are operating in Hindus five hundred years ago, Ancient Mexicans a thousand years ago, or Ancient Egyptians many thousands of years ago. All these works exhibit similar characteristics, slow rhythms of great nicety built of suave forms in conglobate arrangements.

127

62. EASTER ISLAND. Polynesian figure (British Museum)

63. Ancient
Egyptian:
colossal head in
granite
(British
Museum)

64. Ancient Egyptian: seated figure in granite (British Museum)

65. Ancient Central American ritual mask (British Museum)

66. Assyrian, ninth-century B.C. Colossal lion, one from a pair flanking a doorway (British Museum Crown Copyright)

67. SANCHI. *Torso of Bodhisatva* (Victoria & Albert Museum, Crown copyright)

68. IVAN MESTROVIC. *Girl with Guitar* (Courtesy of the Trustees, Tate Gallery)

135

PLATES

SECTION TWO
Softer, mainly limestone

In this, the second section of the plates, are assembled those sculptures in a softer stone, mainly limestone, to which the sculptor responds by working them right to the finish with a chisel and hammer. Stones with this texture cannot be made to give anything by rasping, grinding or attempting to polish them; but more than this, under such treatment they become lifeless and inexpressive. They call for an approach in which the sculptor incises upon them with chisel and hammer, records of his most spontaneous and lively gestures. As the reader turns over the plates he will see how the more characteristic passages in these works sparkle from the inspired chisel strokes, unblurred as they are by the hesitant modifications emanating from tame half-heartedness. As the preponderance of the illustrations shows, this kind of vision and feeling for softer stone had its apotheosis during the Romanesque Period in northern Europe. On the other hand, the half-length figure from Honduras shows how men of other races, and in quite other circumstances, can experience a surprisingly similar feeling of the relationship between stone and form.

69. HONDURAS. Ancient half-length figure in limestone
(British Museum, Crown Copyright)

0. Byzantine, relief in marble. This sculpture and the two following of the same set are of unknow
provenance. These three interesting and beautiful reliefs, having been recovered from an even earli
building demolished or ruined were re-used by being incorporated in the old 'Little' Metropolis
Athens when it was built sometime between the ninth and twelfth centuries.

71. Byzantine, relief in marble. One of a set (*see* fig. 70)

72. Byzantine, relief in marble. One of a set (*see* fig. 70)

73. Winchester Cathedral. *Madonna and Child*. English Medieval, in limestone

74. CHARTRES CATHEDRAL. Portrail Royal, N. portal figures in limestone, (Courtauld Institute of Art)

75. CHARTRES CATHEDRAL. Portrail Royal, N. portal detail of figure in limestone (Courtauld Institute of Art)

76. CHARTRES
CATHEDRAL.
Tympanum
sculpture in lime-
stone from the
Portrail Royal
(Courtauld
Institute of Art)

WESTMINSTER ABBEY
English medieval figure in limestone

78. SOUILLAC. French Romanesque figure in limestone

79. ERIC GILL. *Prospero and Ariel*, limestone (Courtesy Trustees of the Tate Gallery)

80. MARK BATTEN. *Allegorical head* in Craigleith (grit-stone)

PLATES

SECTION THREE
Marble and allied stones

In the following third section of the plates are put those sculptures whose style emanates from the processes of working a kind of stone which is soft enough and strong enough to be pierced and deeply cut away; stones which in relation to their hardness are the strongest and least brittle. These are, in fact, the marbles and alike stones. They are the ones that can be drilled away with rotating drills, carved into attenuated bridging and the utmost of free-standing parts of which any stone will allow. Their dense and close-grained texture shows its best surface qualities when rasped, ground or polished.

In the earlier examples, work by Greek sculptors of the sixth century B.C., this style is seen emerging from the style characteristic of the first section, the hard stone section. This is because the introduction of iron, or primitive steel tools, was in the process of taking marble, as a material for sculpture, out of the class of the hard stones. At the opposite end, the Michelangelo sculptures of the Renaissance Period show that by then the advanced state of tool steel permitted every liberty to be taken with marble. After the time of Michelangelo a period set in in which such stone carving as was then being done sought to imitate the kind of forms and designs which can better and more appropriately be generated by modelling in clay and casting in metal. Sculptors seem to have carried out their designs quite inappropriately in stone only to exhibit their virtuosity.

The four unfinished figures by Michelangelo for the projected tomb of Pope Julius (one as frontis) were selected for their obvious double applicability to this book; for their great qualities as sculpture and for technique, and for the very curious side of the technique they show. Michelangelo was a most strange genius, one who achieved supreme results, although following a perverse technique which outrages all the basic things about stone, both æsthetic and practical. As the un-finished figures show, he attacked the block only from one side and from one point of view. He cut the sculptures out as if drawing in three dimensions. Apart from æsthetic considerations, no stone but that extraordinarily accommodating and kindly material Carrara marble would have permitted even him to succeed in such an abuse of mechanical considerations. He grew up in a marble mason's yard and worked only in Carrara marble all his life which helps, to some extent, to account for this peculiar attitude and technique.

81. Greek, sixth century B.C. Relief in marble from frieze of Treasury of Siphonos at Delphi

82. Greek, sixth century B.C. Archaic female figure in marble

83. Greek, early fifth century B.C. Figure in marble, Kouros

84. Greek, fifth century B.C. Figure of Apollo from Olympia, in marble

85. Greek, fifth century B.C. From the Temple of Zeus at Olympia, in marble

86. Greek, fifth century B.C. From the Temple of Zeus at Olympia, in marble

87. Greek, fifth century B.C. Group from Olympia in marble

88. Greek, fifth century B.C. Figure seated, from Olympia, in marble

89. Greek, Hellenistic period. From the Theatre of Dionysus at Athens, in marble

90. Greek, late Classical period. Athens, marble

91. MICHELANGELO.   Unfinished figure for projected tomb
of Pope Julius, in marble.

92. MICHELANGELO. Unfinished figure for projected tomb
of Pope Julius, in marble